THE
LONG
WEEPING

Portrait Essays

THE
LONG
WEEPING

Portrait Essays
by

JESSIE VAN EERDEN

ORISON
BOOKS

The Long Weeping: Portrait Essays
Copyright © 2017 by Jessie van Eerden
All rights reserved

ISBN 978-0-9964397-5-6

Orison Books
PO Box 8385
Asheville, NC 28814
www.orisonbooks.com

Distributed to the trade by Itasca Books
1-800-901-3480 / orders@itascabooks.com
www.itascabooks.com

Cover art: "Ruth: Series 6" by Vince Trimboli. Used by permission of the artist.

Manufactured in the U.S.A.

ORISON
BOOKS

Contents

For my parents

Nothing is present...except this one being, but it implicates the whole world.

—Martin Buber, *I and Thou*

Prologue

I stand at the hand pump in the grove, young, maybe ten, having run from the signs of dying. Under the small shingled roof on the cement slab, the iron pump is smudged by creatures that licked it in the night, raccoons and cats and the rumored black bear. My jelly shoes are too tight over my ankle socks and the downy hair on my legs prickles up. The spring chill lingers in that threshold of time, when the daffodils darken and the lilacs begin to make everything sweet and wet. Church has let out now, and tall tired people spill into the churchyard, but I slipped out in the middle of the closing prayer, with Matthew who pumps the handle, banging it against its base, coaxing the deep water to spout in the basin and arc higher and higher to my lips. I know he and I probably love each other, like two animals that trust one another's dusty smell. His body is simply like mine in height, in muscle, though his face is more like a baby's and so he acts mean to seem older, but he wears meanness as if he has wrapped himself in a gauzy curtain, spun around and around, and made off with it: a boy pumping water in his see-through costume of meanness for a girl afraid of the signs of dying.

One sign is the divot in the pillow on the camphor-smell bed that the women murmur about—somebody's mother with a long gray braid left a skull's impression like the bear-impress in the leaf pile in the grove where it is said to sleep. Another sign is the man going blind singing only what he remembers of the hymns, another is hipbone grinding hipbone with no cartilage to quiet the sound, another is each leg caked in pantyhose that plaster over the blue-veined skin that still breaks out at the sleeve, on the hands. And then there's the balding head or the limp hair trying to remember its home perm and the dead jobs that do not pay enough because there are signs someone is taking money from the till at the Wash 'n Shop to get skirt sets for her girls, the girls just a little smaller than me, holding hands going to the church outhouse with lattice around it and air fresheners and tiny spiders weaving homes in the surplus toilet paper tube hollows. Maybe these girls are running too, I know my sister has run—by now she has made it to the car, finally free to scratch the itchy pits she has begun shaving, in a sleeveless dress not fit for the chill and so she jams her arms into the snap-up jean jacket, a hand-me-down from one of the girls bigger than me. My sister has stolen the keys from our mother's purse, she turns the ignition to hear Casey Kasem's countdown, to let the radio pull her into the world, toward names like Madonna and Prince and away from the old names: Harold, Don, Eliza, Gaye, Debbie, Sue, Walter, Jean. The seat's vinyl must be cool on her legs, the steering wheel sure in her grip, and something is saying to her, Don't waste any time getting here, to where the living are, in the world of the radio and *Seventeen Magazine* where no one is old or wears polyester dresses, where your life will finally begin.

I turn to the spouting stream that Matthew has conjured with strength that equals my own. He is still pumping the handle, his baby face ruddy, his thoughts unknown to me. Briefly, both of us watch the miracle at the spout that comes from the deep aquifer where snow has drenched down and seeped past dormant trillium roots, down past worm and centipede burrows, into networks of sandstone and clay, slate and sediment, to a breathspace that opens for water to pool in secret. For the rest of my life I will remember the taste of the water that says, Don't waste time on water that is not water, on thirst that is not thirst.

The churchyard people will soon be heavy with egg noodles and beef, a still and lacquered afternoon when flies buzz, naps like dying-practice (for the rest of my life I will fear the death-kernel in naps and will wear myself out like a flapping terrified bird only to push through afternoons). I bend to the stream of water that meets my lips, and right then, with my face in the small echo chamber of the basin, I hear my name, Jess, called from the water. I'm startled and I shoot up and look around. I hear it again, this time from the gravel lot across the road. It's my sister standing beside the car, sullen in the lilac-wet, in the jean jacket, draining the battery to listen to the radio. She hollers for me again. She must want to leave, or must want me to hear the top hit. All at once I long for her and long for the water, too, and cannot help but bend to the iron basin again with its cobwebs now made visible by the water and sagging, the basin with tiny bug bodies and leaves. And still it seems that my name has come from the water spout, as if the water itself has named me and known me already, and I am small and not my own, not some new creature who has lit out and escaped, not so unlike the ones dying. Soon Matthew will push me aside for his turn, his shove the only way we ever know how to touch, but I am bending and drinking again, the water so cold, and I drink the name given to me, so cold I am startled again. Soon I will barrel down the little hill to the tinny car radio to crowd into the driver's seat beside my sister's body and hear the top hit, but I feel like weeping. I drink and I drink.

Woman with Spirits | *Eliza*

We photograph things in order to drive them out of our minds.
My stories are a way of shutting my eyes.

—Kafka

Eliza, you sat with Don on the porch swing that the Catholics built, and you looked at the camera dead center. This was before I was born and before I had my own bout with ambivalence for the place we were from in West Virginia, and for the way I couldn't get my breath sometimes when I left to sleep over at a friend's place in town. Though it happened before I was born, Mom told me that Jessie Beatty Shaffer had told it to her, with a fire in her eyes, insisting that we know because we were Don's relation through Dad's mother if you went back far enough.

Jessie said President Johnson's photographers came combing through Appalachia in the Sixties, trying to capture on film the justification for Johnson's War on Poverty. Everybody in the Whetsell Settlement was furious over how they snuck in and took shots of your curtained-off toilet, the tobacco juice blotting the floor because Don didn't always use a spittoon, the huge pots for bathwater on the stove, the skinny spigot over the sink that trickled and sometimes stopped altogether in winter till someone from Beatty Church would take a turn going over to thaw the pipes. The photographers came, Jessie said, and took their pictures, and never asked much about you and never came back.

I came to know you after all that. I rode over with Mom in the truck through both of Butch's cattle gates, with applesauce and your mail. Once, during a visit, I handed you a potholder, wrapped as a present; I don't know why I gave it to you. I think it had to do with my fear of Don and my shame. When we took you and Don to church some Sundays and Don jabbed at the toes of my patent leather shoes with his cane and said things I couldn't make out, he smiled as though it were a game he played and you stood by and shook your head. I thought he seemed more like your child than your husband.

You stayed in that sloping house for decades, making do on welfare checks that maybe embarrassed you. You stayed even after Butch got the property from Don for a pittance and left you only lifetime rights to the house, and even after Don died and you were too old to bank your own fires. You stayed though you knew that an ambulance could never make it up the road to you if you needed it in winter.

You took years of convincing to finally move to an apartment in Kingwood, with carpet and a hot shower. All those years when you lived down the road from me, I squinted at you with my young eyes and I didn't understand you and I loved the cheap sheer pink scarves you wore on your head for church.

Though I suspect the photographers were well-meaning—reckoning the sacrifice of your dignity small enough on the scale of the greater good—I resent the way they pressed you into the flat, colorless photo and showed you to the world. Even as a kid, when I heard about it from Mom, I went out to our swing set and swung with a resentment beyond my understanding. And, though I need to be careful with my judgments, I admit that I resent the social-service groups who came, too, in their vans—the VISTAs, the Baptist and Catholic kids from the suburbs—talking to you loud and slow, coming to make good for you and assuming that all you knew was squalor. And yet I also wonder sometimes what it was that kept you living out past Butch's two gates for so many years, with a toilet you couldn't flush tissue down, having to burn it in the stove. I wonder if it was habit or stubbornness or love.

I've imagined the scene lots of times. The room would have been so unbelievably still—because you and Don often sat still for a time—that even to fasten a button would be to storm in. And the photographers'

Broncos jostled down the rutted drive, through the cattle gates, and pulled up to your dark, shingle-sided house, with that blond-wood porch swing smarting their eyes. And they eased their way in and their shirt collars chafed in the heat and, as you came out to meet them, they said: Could we get you and your husband on the porch, ma'am? Could we come in? And later, with fewer ma'ams and more imperatives: Draw the water to heat for your bath, like you just did. Yes, and hold it there. I can presume a camera lens coming in close to catch that rub of Copenhagen in your lower lip. In the top right corner, the lens would catch the framed sketch above the sink, a sketch of Ruth who was a gleaner in the Bible, looking bashful with her ephah of barley there above your sink basins. And then the glossy book came, not with your names printed underneath—Don and Eliza Jeffers—but with captions like: *Woman And Man On Porch*, *Woman And Stove*, *Woman With Butter Black From Coal Dust* (a plastic butter dish center-frame, with its lid set down off to the side, and there a black rectangle of butter; then to its left, blurry in the background: a second stove, this one a barreled iron furnace standing as though convicted, guilty of the blackness, its flue outlet not quite flush with the wall as it carries the smoke outside). *Woman With Dog With Mange*, *Woman With Coal Pile*, and so it would have gone, without you ever meeting that Woman on the page.

You never saw yourself in the way they saw you, framed and cropped for a project. (Through the camera lens, could they have possibly seen the thing you told my mother, when she sighed to you once with a tone of pity, about how you never thought caring for Don—with his mind weakened by a boyhood ear infection even when you first met him in his mother's house—was unbearably hard, because you loved him? And you knew you loved him—Even if I just went to the fourth grade, you said, there are still things I know. You said it clearly, and with a hint of reproach.)

Photos expose, but I think this did more than expose. The way Jessie Shaffer told it, with her hackles raised, the photographers bullied and documented you. It was like they shoved away something, someone pitiable, because then the people who would look might say, Yes, pitiable, and might name you a pathetic name of their own making, shut you up inside that name, flatten you into a photo in a book or a file folder, and the pitiable thing would be outside of themselves, something they could overpower and hold in their hand, at arm's length. They'd tsk tsk and give money to get you out of there—because, of course, you would need out of there—you and all the others like you, living in such filth.

But there has to be more to it. I saw you after you moved to the town apartment, where none of the walls leaned in, where the walls were brick. The heat was gas. You had an easy chair. The kitchen sink's silver faucet gleamed. A Scotch-Brite green and yellow sponge sat in its cellophane wrapper on the counter by the sink, and your eyes looked lost, like they'd fallen back into themselves. And you smelled so clean—not a trace of wood smoke.

***

This thing with you and Don—the way the photographers swept through—it stays with me and works into me now and again, as I move about the world and note the way people look at each other. Sometimes the resentment still boils up. I am trying to get a handle on it.

I took a trip once, in a summer of my early twenties, the first time I ever left the country, my young blood racing. I traveled to Moldova in Eastern Europe to visit my friend Nicole who was teaching English there. This was after you and Don had both died—Don first when they wouldn't release him from the hospital and his heart broke from homesickness and stopped; and then you a few years later in your apartment in Kingwood. This was after I left home for school and after Butch's son took over the trailer and the two cattle gates.

Moldova is a poor country, hilly farmland, and most of the villages still keep outhouses like the one I was accustomed to at Beatty Church—no crisp flush, the cobwebs and curled dead leaves in the corner. In the cities, the Moldovan women wore heels and skin-tight jeans and eye makeup, but in the villages and towns, I saw simple polyester dresses, kerchiefs like the ones you wore to church, and the people there flashed a look that was familiar to me, a look of learned—and then gradually instinctive—deference mingled with indignation toward outsiders.

The first week I was there, Nicole and I, and her Moldovan friend Valerie, took the small van-like rutierra to the Orthodox monastery in the town of Hîncu. As the rutierra pulled away, we climbed a dirt path to the monastery: the buildings had been painted a pale, giddy yellow with flowerbeds arranged around them as garnishes. Nuns milled through the grounds, carrying buckets and scrunching up their faces like boys sucking on mouthfuls of sour candies. The backdrop of that pale yellow didn't suit the women; they needed ox-blood black, not yellow.

We climbed the steps to the main cathedral, entered the narthex where a nun sold pocketbook icons for a few lei, but were turned away in curt Romanian. Nicole translated to me that the floor was being redone and no one could go in that day. So we walked out through the marigold-garnished footpath to a crucifix icon roofed over with an arc of hammered tin punctured in flowery designs. The near-naked Jesus sagged his head left, a dove alighted on his head, a skull and crossbones propped up his nailed-on feet. His eyes rolled back in his head so I could see only the whites.

I was a churchgoing kid through and through—you know that, Eliza, since my family picked you up some Sundays for worship at Beatty. In the pews of my childhood, I studied the bronze, wavy-haired Jesus pictured beside the pulpit and looking off as he did toward the cord that

Harold pulled to ring the bell, but looking beyond that, too. I was rabid for Jesus, over earnest and sentimental and enfolded. But, right then in Moldova, thousands of miles from my fold, on the grounds of that monastery of nuns and icons, both whose eyes avoided mine, with my Orthodox-costume scarf askew on my head, a nonbelieving bone all at once rattled around inside me. I decided this Jesus icon belonged in LaVade Wilson's yard, down from the Gillespies' in the Settlement, next to the other wild things she put out at Halloween, the scarecrow holding a scythe, the plastic Santa lawn ornament wearing a rubber wolf mask. The thought of LaVade Wilson helped me find my footing for a moment, but it wasn't really comfort that I felt.

Nicole and I headed to the outhouse while Valerie waited for us in the shade. After we stuck what was left of our toilet-paper rolls back into our backpacks, we followed the dirt path to the pool where people could bottle holy water, which the nuns also sold along with fizzy water down by the main road. But the holy water spring must have run dry or something, since a large off-road truck sat parked alongside it, revving, sprouting a hose that led down into the dry reservoir. A young Moldovan man in dress clothes, looking at our backpacks and jeans, asked in English if we were American. Without waiting for our reply, he said we must stay for the special prayer that was to take place at noon. His dark eyes looked hungry, and though he said nothing else to us, we felt compelled to stay. The rutierra wouldn't come back for us for a couple of hours anyway. We followed the path around to another monastery building where Valerie was waiting, across from the cathedral and LaVade Wilson's sorry Jesus, and we sat together on the steps till noon, watching some Moldovan city women, who'd come on the rutierra with us, pose for photos in their dresses and heels against the pale yellow of the cathedral. And right at noon, the prayer service started within the monastery hall behind us.

It began as a priest's low murmur. Then, at intervals, his Romanian jumped an octave into a shout. We stayed outside on the steps, nervous and quiet, as more and more people crowded in behind us. Soon, and without much warning, the summer day was torn by howling and weeping from inside the hall. I could hear a woman, whimpering and shrieking, off and on, in between whatever the priest shouted, and I saw the Moldovan man rush in, shooting us an eager glance. After a while, Valerie told us in halted English that it was an exorcism and that the woman had come for prayer. The priest was ridding her of a spirit. Valerie shifted her weight till she finally went in. Nicole and I sat as though pinned to the steps, with nothing to look at but the Jesus icon under its tin roof. I shut my eyes.

***

But, Eliza, I didn't shut my eyes because all of this was foreign, though I knew the Moldovan man didn't assume an exorcist past on our part. Instead, it held an eerie familiarity. It was pushing me to understand something, but I didn't know what exactly. I knew that as a little girl in the Settlement, I'd heard the story of Christ casting the unclean spirits out of a man who roamed the caves and cut himself with stones. Jesus sent the demons out into a herd of swine, and I knew a couple of people who tried to follow suit—like the Beatty pastor, the Reverend Joe, who wouldn't wear glasses because he believed God would heal his eyes. He came once to the hospital when my brother Luke had encephalitis and was sick with seizures, and the man tried to exorcise Luke, right there in the hospital room, till Mom asked him to leave.

And one summer my two brothers and my sister and I listened wide-eyed as a demon was cast out of a girl over the radio. We were teenagers, and every day that summer, we tuned in to Bob Larson's radio show "Talk Back" at two in the afternoon on WAJR. On the girls' side of a long upstairs room, we huddled around the single working speaker of a hand-me-down stereo that Uncle Todd brought us from Ohio. We'd heard about Larson from Barry, the evangelist who preached the chapels that summer at Aldersgate Camp up in Cranesville. Barry was from Pittsburgh and he'd brought some Pittsburgh kids to the camp, girls who wore makeup and threaded their fingers through their hair and dropped their jaws at the camp's outdoor bathhouses. Barry ignited us when he preached; he rallied in us what we called a work of the Holy Spirit but what also gave us a sense of self, a kind of access to a spiritual power that we could wield in a world in which we were scruffy and insignificant. An actual world in which we received, not a fierce laying-on-of-hands, like Barry talked about, but a hand-me-down stereo from our uncle who had money in Ohio.

As Bob Larson took his callers, we assumed positions of the stunned devout: we lay on our stomachs, clenching bed pillows; we hugged our knees and leaned against the attic door. Larson mostly preached against Satanic cults and rock music and asked for money. But he had us rapt; he had a voice that raked through our minds, snagging on a knot of doubt now and then, and it hurt when he pulled at the knot because he had bravado. He had sugary pity (for the weepy callers) and fiery, righteous anger (for the lost callers in denial). And he had us hanging on his every word.

When Larson got the call from a girl possessed with a demon, we went rigid. She whimpered into the phone about rape and beatings and then started wheezing and, in a throaty voice, made death threats, which never cowed Larson—he shouted back at the girl, and the static over the phone lines or in the speakers crackled like fire, and he did battle with her evil spirit right there on the air. He named the spirit Legion because he said there were many in her, tormenting her, he said in the name of Jesus, in the name of Jesus, leave her, and the girl groaned. She came out of it with a weak, puppy voice, dripping with gratitude and tears, as he kept stroking her with his voice, promising her pamphlets in the mail and his newsletter. Larson came out of it with a few donations.

I faced the stereo speaker and shut my eyes tight, imagining this girl who seemed like she would have white-bluish skin, papery skin that showed every bruise, and she glistened with sweat and sat alone and held her own hands.

Jess, Jake said to me, you don't have to be afraid. You're a believer. But he didn't sound convinced himself—we were young and defenseless in our upstairs room, still listening as an ad came on. I was afraid, but I wasn't as afraid as I was longing to know who the girl really was, what she looked like and why she'd called in and if, when she hung up the phone, she cried, or sat still, or what. Larson took another caller, someone abused by Satanists, someone who said he had eaten a ceremony victim's heart—which segued into a pitch for more money—then someone hosting another band of demons, someone calling from a shabby room with a single-bulb light.

I remembered this girl's radio voice when the shrieking and thrashing started in that Moldovan monastery, in the hall behind me, and I remembered you, Eliza, and it was that same resentment that I felt. Anybody could tell by the woman's screaming that she suffered. And anybody could tell that the priest's voice was raking through her, in the heat of incense and icons, with prayers in a tongue I didn't understand but with a merciless force I knew something about. And, Eliza, she seemed to me defenseless and, in that crowd, she seemed alone.

***

I have tried, these past few years, to find those pictures they took of you and Don. I've searched in books and archives and libraries, but never found them. The closest I came was a photo taken in 1935 in Terra Alta, up on the mountain a few miles from where we lived. I found it in the magazine *Art in America,* and the article said the photo was taken by Walker Evans who was one of FDR's photographers commissioned to drum up public support for Roosevelt's New Deal during the Depression by taking pictures. In the photograph, a girl wearing a middy blouse with puffy sleeves and a sequined party hat reaches out her hand to touch or point to something outside of the photo's frame. Beside her, an older, shorter woman wears a heavy coat with a fur collar (even though it's July), and clutches a tissue or maybe a coin purse to her chest. The article said that on July 4, 1935, New York photographer Walker Evans entered Terra Alta, West Virginia, and during the town's festivities, photographed these two women and, thereafter, filed their faces under his name in the Library of Congress as "Independence Day, Terra Alta, West Virginia, 1935 July, gelatin silver print." Evans helped give American poverty a visible face, said the article, but in his diary on the day he took this picture, Evans wrote:

> In end of rain to Terra Alta pronounced Teralta. There a homecoming of natives, very degenerate natives, mush faced, apathetic, the pall of ignorance on all sides. Photographed the most gruesome specimens.

I read and reread what Evans wrote and I felt again that resentment, even fury. I'm not not foolish enough to deny the marks of the poverty of that time—the marks even remained when I was a girl in the Eighties spending every July Fourth in Teralta at my great-aunt Becky's along the parade route. It was a railroad town and, of course, the railroad boom had shriveled to a joke. Across the street from Becky's place, a house lined its railing with fake flowers and propped up its porch roof with two-by-fours. I remember that it always rained, and I loved the rain, and I felt love for that place. But even if I hadn't gone there as a little girl and felt a particular pride, the fury would still rise up—and that fury is becoming clearer to me—because, commissioned as he was, Evans wielded his camera with a power that the people in front of his lens didn't have. He framed and cropped their suffering, forced it into a black-and-white record, and claimed for himself a private knowledge of them—that violent kind of knowledge that says: I own you, I clutch you like you clutch that coin purse, there is nothing new or strange in you that I don't already know and haven't already risen above, there is, in fact, no bloom in you, and it's a pity. He gave no thought to the middy-blouse girl's mind as a thing layered like an onion, like a rose. He did not accord her the weeping and the exulting, the prismatic experience of sunlight that Evans certainly maintained for himself in his own complexity. He doomed the girl in her party hat and, by doing so, drove her out, away from him, left her alone, and at the same time, he drove out his own vulnerable fear that he may have had about things falling apart, the world falling apart, and about how he might as well turn to the wall when that happened.

President Johnson's war started when the poverty of the Thirties rusted into the poverty of the Sixties. In 1964, Lyndon and Lady Bird Johnson climbed onto a sagging porch in Inez, Kentucky, and in front of TV cameras he said: I have called for a national war on poverty. Our objective: total victory. And the photographers again went searching, in shacks and slums and down roads with two cattle gates, to find the poor and shove them into the light for the others to see and make claims on. To shove people onto a path of redemption, of clean carpets, hot showers, huge-pipe sinks, and silent, well-ordered rooms.

Eliza, you had a single-bulb pantry, with a narrow window, before you moved to Kingwood. It was a pretty pantry, I remember, you said so yourself. Liz, when she went to work work for the Senior Center, came over from her house a couple of miles away, and helped you put contact paper on all the shelves to put the canned goods on, and also some of those old Ball jars of blue glass, overturned and beautiful in the window light. The contact paper was white with tiny purple flowers in three different phases of blossoming: bud to full-face to bending and bent with petals closing up. The pantry walls leaned toward the center from the weight of split firewood stacked against the other side of the wall. You finished it before dark, so Liz could make it back home for supper, down the hill a ways, down her driveway pocked like a dry riverbed, her chickens loose among the ducks.

If the photographers would have come again, they might have made that picture, of you in your pantry not very full. And who would have been able to tell the purple of the flowers or the blue of the jars in a black-and-white picture, and who would have known that Liz had helped and that you had listened to music on the radio while you worked at it, and that there were days you spent, when it was warm in the sun by the window, arranging, till they suited you, the canned beets that people in the Settlement gave you, and the soups and the beans. The team of photographers might still have assumed your apathy, your ignorance—but then, I am not being careful with my judgment. I am speaking out of fury, knowing that fury can have the same source as love. And I am still learning how to temper them both.

✳ ✳ ✳

All that is to say, when the Moldovan woman in a kerchief and a simple polyester housedress, this exorcised woman followed by a throng of other kerchiefed women, carried her cries outside of the monastery and sent them up against the lovely yellow of the shut-up cathedral's outer walls—I felt inexplicable fury and no longer nervousness. Of course there were things I didn't understand about the rite of this foreign culture, but I was helplessly furious with the priest's strong-arming all the same, and also somehow furious with myself, how I only sat there.

She lay on the floor of the porch and flopped like a hurt fish until she went limp. All was quiet and she only twitched now and then, until someone from the crowd took her arm and led her away. The priest was nowhere. I never did get a look at him. All of the other winded believers slowly shuffled past LaVade Wilson's Jesus, crossing themselves. And all throughout the exorcism, over by the cathedral, those women in heels kept posing in front of the yellow, in a Marilyn Monroe forward bend, grinning despite the shrieks.

So, the man in dress clothes came over and said to us on the steps, nodding toward the porch where the woman had fish-flopped, If you don't see this, then you don't believe. And he brushed his hands together, as though finishing a job.

That's not true, I actually said, fuming beyond reason, foolish and feeling ignorant and wanting to say something sensible about what had happened, that there had to be more to it, but he wasn't listening. He was crossing himself mechanically in front of the same icon that I had begun to hate for its grasp on the people who passed by it.

The woman's howls, still hanging in the air, were like imagined things in my mind. I guessed the howling was supposed to be the sound of the demon as it left, an evil spirit driven out, flapping its monstrous wings and fleeing—like Legion leaving the girl who dissolved into drivel on the radio at the command of Bob Larson.

***

I remember the remaining shell of the exorcised woman as she trembled and faltered on the monastery's footpath. I can't say what she felt. But you, Eliza, come into my mind, vivid like a vision, though not fiery. Just clear. I think of you offered up to the camera, like to a priest—undefended—subject to the lens peering in, and it's as though someone said, with smugness: I know all about your soul. The photographers, the priests, they look at a face as if by looking they can grasp and know—they name the demon and cast it out, they frame the guilty stove and the pouched lip in a photo and call it poverty, call you poor, call the sorrow Legion, and purge it all out, but there is more blooming there than they can ever know.

Something still shook the kerchiefed woman whose demons had already up and fled, but I felt like we all, on the monastery's porch, cowered from it. Maybe the woman felt she had needed a priest's prayer and holy water, or maybe someone else had presumed her need, just as someone presumed what you needed, urging you toward a move to town, to a hot shower, even when you said, I've been sponge-bathing for seventy years, why would I need a hot shower now? Even when you could mourn Don in that shingle-sided house in ways you couldn't anywhere else, in that place where your curtain-walls hung and smoke worked into the folds of cloth and skin.

I have, I guess, no dread of demons, though I once did. I do have dread of our mishandling of one another, and the shoving we do of one another's souls as though our souls were clods of dirt—how we can abandon one another to our sorrow, shut one another up into it, though we often do it with great shows of helping, always with these great shows and programs and prayer services and claims on redemption. Maybe our abandonment is most frightful when veiled by these compassionate shows. Might it be that when you hurt, something in you opens, and the pain takes root and takes prominence, and if I allow it its root, acknowledge it in you, and come to you powerless, with no commands, and sit with you if you want me to, something in me might open, too, some fuller dimension of your private suffering?

***

A small girl walked by Nicole and me as we sat on the steps of the monastery. Over her little energetic body she wore a rust-red skirt and magenta top. The mismatched skirt-set hung a bit loose. Maybe a hand-me-down. She moved without shyness; she moved with her whole self. When she looked right at me as she stole past, I was finally able to cry. She held something stubborn in her—running like a lion down the path—something discordant and strange, with some quality in her that refused to be known. I was sick for home and sick for this girl's defiance—it was there in you, too, there despite it all—defiance toward anybody's pronouncements, toward even a written portrait like this that, in its best effort, is still a kind of containment, failing in the face of your resistance. And it's good that it fails. I just wanted to write you, to tell you, that I don't need to find those photos to see you.

I can shut my eyes and see you, beyond the edge of a photograph. The deep rut lines on your face full of coal smoke, your hands gone soft ever since you couldn't lift the firewood. Your nails that Liz sometimes painted. The crevasse of both worry and welcome between your brows. Your bent back. Your secret light stealing now and then across your eyes. The syringes and the SSI checks and the half-eaten cup of cottage cheese on the table all insisting: I'm here. I shut my eyes and see your yellow AM/FM radio, its antenna straining toward the window like a gladiola stem, and you hold the shabby thing in your hands and look at me.

This Soul Has Six Wings | *The Beguines*

The way I see it, a mystic takes a peek at God and then does her best to show the rest of us what she saw. She'll use image-language, not discourse. Giving an image is the giving of gold, the biggest thing she's got. Mysticism suggests direct union, divine revelation, taking a stab at the Unknown with images, cryptic or plain, sensible or sensory. A mystic casts out for an image in whatever is at her disposal and within reach, like a practiced cook who can concoct a stew from the remaining carrots, a bruised potato, or like a musician improvising with buckets and wooden spoons. She does not circumvent; she hammers a line drive. A mystic is a kid finding kingdom in the ash heap.

The thirteenth-century Beguine mystics were women with their eyelids licked open by God, like those of monkey-faced puppies. These women seemed slipped into history, or in between histories. Though their only options were marriage or the cloister, they carved out a new option by forming quirky spiritual communities, out from under the rule of men or monastic structure. They spanned about a hundred years and covered some ground circulating a few manuscripts before they were married off or shuffled into approved orders. The lay women's movement spread like a brushfire over northern Europe. Women grouped into Beguinages, small cities within cities. Some of the larger ones, like the Beguinage of Ghent hosting a thousand women, had a church, cemetery, hospital, streets. They cropped up on the outskirts of cities in the Netherlands, Belgium, Germany. The women took no conventional vows. They were free to leave the community to marry; some brought their children. They retained private property; they didn't beg; they did manual work for pay. They had no founder, no common rule that dictated community life. And no signing or changing your name.

Wars of the thirteenth century left a surplus of solitary women, and made way for the pop religion upsurge: meetings dotted the hillsides like Baptist tent revivals. Women made up the majority of the penitent, and many sought a fulltime religious life, flocking to the doors of Cistercian Orders, but denied access. This huge batch of proselytes was sniffing out a Way beyond a doctrine. In 1175 Lambert le Bègue, a sympathetic priest of Liège in Belgium, encouraged a group of lay women to form an independent religious community. Their main tenets were voluntary poverty and freedom. They held fast to the Eucharist and the humanity of Jesus; they were chaste and charitable and unpopular with most parish priests. They came to be known as the Beguines.

The surviving texts of the Beguine mystics deliver image-language in the form of allegory and dialog and lyric. A Beguine named Margaret Porette wrote the controversial text *The Mirror of Simple Souls* in the French vernacular, personifying Love, the Soul, and Reason. She claimed that a human soul can be joined at the hip with God through love: This Soul, says Love, has six wings, just as the Seraphim. She no longer wishes for anything which comes by an intermediary, for that is the proper state of being of the Seraphim; there is no intermediary between their love and God's love. She taught the soul's annihilation: that the soul, in Holy Church the Greater, might have no will of her own, that she might serve only as a mirror for God's image and will. Porette's book was burned publicly by the Bishop of Cambrai, but she made no concessions. In fact, she added seventeen more chapters, moved her allegory forward, spruced up her characters. She got burned at the stake in 1310.

Another main text came out of Germany: *Flowing Light of the Godhead* by Mechthild of Magdeburg. Her first manuscript is in the low-German dialect and draws on images from courtly love, a secular tradition. Mechthild admits: I do not know how to write nor can I, unless I see with the eyes of my soul and hear with the ears of my eternal spirit and feel in all the parts of my body the power of the Holy Spirit. And, to convey the Spirit, she uses what's available, what she sees out her window, touches to her lips, knows in her body.

A mystic is unapologetic for a lack of theological education, a scholar's explanations. (Porette: You must let Love and Faith together be your guides to climb where Reason cannot come.) The Beguines' writings depict common tropes of spiritual literature: a bride, a desert, a bed of pain. These images trigger something in me. What if I cast about for my own, for things that have caught my attention the way a fence barb does a loose shirt? What if that's all you have? Just the images? Perhaps images leave room or make room for mystery. Image as a felt truth for the weak who need more than doctrine. You struggle for an image; it wriggles into life and is born.

Is there a place for the contemporary mystic? Can someone try again to crawl into the big shell of mystical tradition and holler and hear her small voice echo back? Can she reclaim it in some way?

The way I see it, a mystic simply believes that God visits.

A mystic stays with what's striking: past the windshield, in between the intermittent wipers, a shadow, a flash of light, color, a face. She sees something, she sees and then she runs to show and tell, or at least she practices speeches in her head. She mulls over her images, arranges her sermon in a picture book—it's like a touch-and-feel kids book, furry cloth for monkey feet, a bit of rubber ball for bear nose. She wants her images vivid.

The Beguines had two main takes on the image of the desert. Some references pointed to the wilderness where the Old Testament children of Israel wandered for forty years, in exile, in desperation, trying to make it to the promised land of milk and honey. Life is exile, according to these writings. Life is the trial to be endured, the soul's desolate journey home to God. The other manifestation of the desert image is an encounter: the desert isn't the thing to be endured for the goal; it is the goal; it is the landscape of union. It is, from the Book of Hosea, the place where God will allure her, bring her into the wilderness, and speak comfort to her. It's where you learn how to love.

A burned-down trailer is a desert of ash, silt, secrets. It is exposure, down to the ground, to wind to sun to rain. Brought to nothing. A melted photograph here, a charred, unfastened locket there. A blackened mirror.

A fencerow, attended by walnut and hickory trees, separated my house from Christie's trailer. Before the trailer burned, Christie and I made a break in the fence so she could come to my side and I could go to hers.

A grease fire on the stove. It was in late fall. My brother Luke and I were just returning from a walk. We'd seen a deer close-up, licking water from the streambed. We had been silent with it and after it quenched its thirst, it picked its way through the underbrush into the cloak of the pines. We were heading back when we saw the huge piles of black smoke stacking on top of the bare trees. The trailer seemed to burn clear to the ground in minutes. Nobody was caught inside, and they even got some of the clothes out. But Christie and her younger brother G.W. were standing outside, close to the fence, with smoky blank faces. They seemed exposed there to the wind and the bits of ash flaking down like dirty snow. From my front porch, I stood watching her home become nothing.

What happens, Christie, when you lose everything? I picture that charred trailer-desert in my head now, remembering how they stayed for a time up at Nolan Wilson's old place and how we gave bags of clothes and a Glow Worm that lit up when you pressed him, trying to fill their new nothing. In the beginning, there was a home with rooms and maybe not plenty but at least something, and then there was wasteland, no-place, no-home.

What happens when you lose everything? When you slip out, down the chain-link fire escape ladder and leave all evidence of self behind in the rubbish? Sometimes I think I want to choose it, to try to learn emptiness, a trailer-desert, a sigh in the soul. But I don't know that I could.

Why speak in images? In trailer fire? What's the point when they leave you winded and unsure? Well, you don't know what else to say, or how else to say it, like holding the hand of someone who's lost everything. It is an inexplicable being-with, a fleshing, and a new way.

Is a mystic anyone who realizes a truth and flashes it, like a strong poker hand? She is maybe the checkout lady at the Dollar General, talking on the phone to her husband who's trying to get the title for the truck but can't read the forms, can't read at all, he needs her, and she has to get off—there are customers. And she realizes and she says, This is all too much. On her face you see clearly where her weeping goes. You remember exactly what she looks like.

A neighbor calls in early evening about the double rainbow in the sky. Another and another calls, Judy, Aunt Kathy from town. From the porch, we can see the full arc of one, the marvelous ghost of the other. We have not lost this need to tell, to show, to point.

Sometimes you see nothing in the sky, no promises or marks of Jesus's feet, no sign that he's coming back to bring you home—so you write the nothing and the no-place, too.

Beguines weren't recluses. Uncloistered, they grouped their small cabins together into their Beguinages on the outskirts of cities where they worked making lace or gardens, teaching or nursing, managing shelters for urban women and kids who worked in textiles. Their cabins made a half-circle; one could see the other's light from her stoop, could string together two tin cans, window to window. Out from this half-circle shelter, Beguine mystics attracted the urban faithful, with their penchant for heresy and the use of the vernacular, the tongue of fire making sense. They gathered in the exiled and wandering. They had a context for dealing with suffering.

In my mid-twenties, for a time, I gathered with a group of women in Philadelphia, all of us assembling around Jesus, like girls hovering around a radio. As you hover in a circle, you brush arms with each other. Lisa was a woman among us whose husband was incarcerated, and she had three boys and a tiny frame; she looked like she could blow away. And still, she beautifully braced herself under her heavy beam of a dadless series of days that bore down with the weight of her boys' birthdays, street hockey games, piss-in-the-bed nights. Nobody skirted around her; we entered in as best we could.

We met in Susan's house in Hunting Park, always ending up in the kitchen. We ate and then sang a few choruses and discussed Scripture. One night it was James's epistle in the New Testament: Count it all joy, he says, when you fall into various trials, knowing that the testing of your faith produces patience. We cried onto our plates of Spanish rice and chicken that Blanca had brought, because the trials were various: Wendy's husband left her and the kids, another husband had cancer, Celeste and her girls lost their row house, Maria had a heating bill she could not pay.

Often, a woman takes tentative steps toward another, shy about the magnetic pull of this other's wounds. A raw, undisguised wound pulls you out of your own general okayness: your safe bed, your comfort. There is something about her uncontained and spilling-out life, a doll losing its fiber-fill, the dazed hungry look of one knocked off course. You want to zip up the back of her dresses, paint your lips together with Bonnie Bell Cranberry, and borrow her wakefulness that came the moment her husband left. You feel that you've been drawn away from your life so that you can miss it for the first time, so you can see it and knock out its walls and shiver, alive again, as though you've taken a dip in ice-cold water.

But is it a longing for laceration? That extreme mystical asceticism or mortification of flesh and the wakefulness it affords? Or, is it maudlin, sentimental?

I don't think so. I don't think that's what it was for most of the Beguines. It's simply the fact of suffering, the dealing with it, making meaning out of it, and if there is no meaning, just to share it.

Here's my image: a gathering in the kitchen, a group bound to each other. A girl slips in, slides down the wall to sit hugging her knees on the linoleum—she has missed a period, or she's lost her baby, or her husband's left, or she simply couldn't get out of bed till two in the afternoon. Out the window, the fire hydrant shoots out streams in the Philadelphia July heat and kids gallop this way and that, and she suffers, and the others come around, crowd the kitchen. They bring Spanish rice and chicken, boiled milk for coffee. And the gathered women stay there, through the early fall, into November. They are entering winter together, pointing out the window, Look: how gentle the snow.

I wonder if mystical life is really about visions, or if it's about looking again at the pieces you've already got: of a rocky marriage, a job at Dollar General, a double rainbow. And if you see the kingdom of God there if you stare long enough. I wonder if it's about holding yourself still as a mirror. Or about making a big scene, waving your arms wildly.

There is something dangerous about a mystic.

Held suspect from the beginning for their disregard for ecclesiastical hierarchy, the unschooled Beguines fell out of favor with the clerics. The women fueled the Church's disapproval by reading biblical texts to everyday folks in their native tongue. In 1274 the Council of Lyons banned any new spiritual orders from forming; new groups had to operate within an existing, approved order. There were rumors of prostitution, sexual license. The Inquisition wasn't kind. In 1312 the Council of Vienne officially declared the Beguines heretical, accusing them of association with antinomian adherents of the Free Spirit. Their property was confiscated; many women had to marry. Many were forced to sign up with a convent.

What's so dangerous about a mystic? Hurling and wielding the best stuff she can imagine, insisting on an unmediated way of wakefulness. A mild heretic with dyed pink hair and a threadbare T-shirt with the slogan *Take me seriously*.

Today, I don't suppose she fears the Inquisition and its fire—just dullness, just missing it. She fears dismissal. She wrestles, she squints the eyes of her soul. Perhaps she doesn't ditch tradition as much as take it for its word and peer inside its cavernous shell. There must still be something worth saying, worth pointing to.

Without | *Simone*

This world is the closed door. It is a barrier, and at the same
time it is the passage-way.

—Simone Weil

My family has joined the Opels at their farm where they raise Cornish
Crosses, large broilers. The fathers have set up operations by the hen-
house: two iron pots of water kept at a boil for scalding the fresh carcasses, a long table for defeathering once the scald has loosened the feather
shafts. The fathers slaughter behind the barn. They string up the clucking
hens by their feet and cut off their heads swiftly with the axe—I'm not
exactly sure how they maneuver it—and we kids, from our stations at
the table, hear the headless bodies flap and swing and fling blood all over
the men's shirtfronts and boots. A few of the heads bounce into our view,
the thin eyelid taking time to slide closed. Once motionless, the bodies
are eased into the boiling water and then my older brothers pull them
onto the long table where we pluck them clean, the nude steaming birds,
then plunge them into buckets of ice. Beside me at the table, Matthew's
face is round and red over the task. He says little, he presses on a naked
broiler's stomach and squeezes out the remaining air in her lungs in a
final squawk, a big ugly voice repeating with each push in a stutter. It's
awful. He is forever a boy I am supposed to love. We eat alongside each
other at Beatty Church potluck meals, we sit side by side in the choir
and sing the Beatitudes from the King James, *Blessed are they which do*
hunger and thirst for righteousness, for they shall be filled, Matthew in his
dreadful tenor. One day, he will be the rural West Virginia boy I did not
marry. After today, we will smell like raw denuded breast for so long.

Elizabeth Opel and I, who weary quickly of pulling stubborn

feathers, are charged with carrying the bodies to the canners, to our mothers. The bodies are upended, we clutch their feet, and the inches are few between the headless necks and the rye grass nuggeted with cold cow manure. I hold a pair of scaly bound feet in each hand as I cross the pasture from the butchering table to the basement kitchen, and I feel, without having the words for it, this dangerous intimacy. I feel gravity in the hens hanging from my hands. I move as quickly as I can through the field, Elizabeth falling behind. I still hear the hen's big voice and I round the corner to the basement door propped open and there are the mothers on the concrete floor with a drain somewhere that makes all the room tilt slightly inward. I search out my mother's face, always a face I feed on just as I fed on her milk, as I fed on her blood-food for nine months. I stand at the open door with a cold carcass in each hand watching the mothers at the stove with the pressure canners and pots and mason jars in the sink, vats of ice, vats of talk, ring lids lined up and ready. Their hands work automatically, they take my burdens without a word, and begin to turn the dead things toward a fate of buttered dish or casserole or tender barbecue. All this intricacy, all the intimate viaducts of feeding swirl toward the floor drain with a violent quiet. I look for the hidden drain, I see blood on my shoes. I spin around as Elizabeth arrives, and run back to where Matthew will be waiting for me.

***

Tonight I return to Simone Weil, a French philosopher of the twentieth century. Some people neither heal nor give solace. They disturb, a fresh slap of cold air through the window when you crawl at midnight to the desk longing for its force of recognition. And once there, beneath the window, you notice it's raining and the rain is slanting in. You smell your lover on you and you smell animal, all body and fur, no ideas, as you unfurl from sleep. A sense of Weil's saintliness wakes your whole self, as the rain darkens the sill, and then you smell only wet wood, picturing her there where you sit, her mind lush and horribly electric in the dark. You picture her notebooks stacked too near the window, getting soggy, the ink running, indecipherable. As if she wants to disappear.

I return to Weil when I remember to wonder how to love without devouring, how to give without harming, how to hold disquieting opposites in the head and abide the contradictions with something like calm. Over the years I've copied out passages from the notebooks she left in the care of Gustave Thibon, the farmer-philosopher who did not respect her wish that he cannibalize her ideas, remove her name as author, and present her thoughts as his own. My copybook is studded with gems attributed rightly to SW, pried out of texts groped for whenever my big shiny life called for them—I the little tornado, the twenty-two-year-old, for instance, in the center of a stack of books, drawn at first glance to Weil's extremity because I was deathly afraid of acquiescing—to what or to whom, I couldn't say. The brightness of her asceticism thrilled me.

Eating—devouring—is a central metaphor in her notebooks, pulled toward God as she was by George Herbert's poem "Love" that ends with the lines: *"You must sit down," says Love, "and taste my meat." / So I did sit and eat*. And, uncomfortably, eating is a central metaphor in her strict life—a stubborn five-year-old refusing sugar because soldiers on the front lines of World War I went without, a thirty-four-year-old philosopher starving herself to death, refusing to eat more than her French countrymen on rations. And so, in 1943, the tuberculosis killed her. Eating is intimacy, devouring is both union with and destruction of what you devour. For Weil this is the crux of ethics and love.

What would she think of the headless hen my younger self held in hand, the hen's big voice? Maybe she would interpret the butchering scene as a pageant of what we often do in loving: behead, denude, plunge, carry like a burden, and feed on. She warned against the violent potential in possessing lover and friend for your own sustenance. The hen's body was a metaphor introduced early to the muscle-memory in my arms, my own warning against such devouring.

It's possible Simone Weil was crazy. She was surely severe and baffling—a Jew who some say hated her Jewishness, a Catholic who refused the sacraments with her heels dug in on behalf of all those outside the fold. A self-denigrating woman in long black capes that hid her hips. A brilliant girl who blazed with such frustration over not being as brilliant a mathematician as her brother that she wanted to die, not out of envy of the glory but out of envy of the access he must have had to truth. She remains a question mark to me mostly, but there's no doubt of one thing: her body was involved with her mind. Her ideas animated her flesh. You see it when she took leave of her teaching post to work the power press at Alsthom Electrical Works in Paris, then to work a milling machine, a stamping press, to feel the factory for a year in her bones and migrainous head. You see it when she rushed to the front of the Spanish Civil War; when she felt, inexplicably, a desire to pray and to do so by kneeling, for what point is there to prayer without bending the body to it?; when she picked grapes with laborers and muttered over and over the Our Father (*the very first words tear my thoughts from my body*); when she demonstrated in the streets with the unemployed and marched with the miners; when she returned to teaching the shy girls with undisciplined thoughts and poor writing skills who helped her fix her misbuttoned sweater. She was a metaphysician who dealt in the physical, nothing mere academic exercise, always zeroing in on the base level of love. So it makes sense she would cultivate an ethic themed by morsel and bread and meat—the stuff of the body.

But it's possible she was too saintly. And it's true she starved herself, really, taking renunciation to suicidal extreme. So why return to such a woman, her radioactive bones showing up through her skin? Because in my everyday life I am trying to love again after failing miserably at it, and I also need to live more responsibly in the world, more generously. But, beyond that, there is an attraction difficult to articulate. I come to her because her aggressive tearing-down of her own ego—her refusal to let it get fat off of the lives of others—inserts a scratchy interruptive sound into the hum of self-satisfaction buzzing around us. There is the publication credit, the slideshow at the college where I teach showing our ranking in *US News & World Report*, there is the quick wit on NPR and the ironic internet meme, there is the sense we are doing well for ourselves and ought to be full of congratulation as we churn out reports on increased enrollment, outcomes met, lives lived successfully and with the appropriate degree of self-awareness. And then there is Simone.

She is there peeling back layers to expose our ravenousness. There is her desire to revoke her very name, there is the transmogrification of her body into bread and meat to be scattered and scraped out the train window to anonymous vine harvesters to whom she may as well have said—Take my notebooks, I am dying—and the workers make their automatic wave to the passing train and then begin, slowly, to gather her in.

***

The first essay I read of hers was "Come with Me." My sister Miss had read it in college and had made me a grainy photocopy from *The Simone Weil Reader*, and I was in love with Miss's experience of college. It's Weil's strange two-page encounter with Christ: *At times he would fall silent, take some bread from a cupboard, and we would share it. This bread really had the taste of bread. I have never found that taste again.* In this same vision, Christ shockingly throws her out onto the stairs of the garret and she wanders the streets trying to gain entry again until she realizes she belongs elsewhere—maybe in a prison cell, she says, or in a suburban house full of knick-knacks. Anywhere but in the garret. And all of her life she seemed to live on that taste, as if to say: Don't waste time on hunger that is not hunger, on bread that is not bread.

When I graduated college and went to work in DC as a stipend volunteer with other fervent volunteers, I got hold of Weil's *Gravity and Grace*. I began my copybook then, in a season of my life when saintliness seemed pragmatic. Late into the night, I typed up passages from the book on a typewriter, annoying Mark who was trying to sleep across the hall because he'd had a long day at the clinic for the homeless. Mark was a caseworker, and I taught high school dropouts. I taped the notes above the desk. *SW: To be only an intermediary between the uncultivated ground and the plowed field, between the data of a problem and the solution, between the blank page and the poem, between the starving beggar and the beggar who has been fed.* Everything in her felt elemental, pungent, poker-hot—it came down to food and feeding, food and love, meat and carnality, what else was there? (I also kissed someone for the first time around then, and kissed three others in the course of a few short months, all of them tasting different.)

Her basic posture seemed to me one of renunciation, of fasting to purify love and to practice not taking bites out of others for your own sustenance. So, I fasted during my volunteer years, a newly minted pacifist during the Iraq War, shortly after the towers went down; I lived with Mennonites who were cradle pacifists. A fast meant letting loose of the material world for a moment so as to make a more vertical reach possible, my hands unoccupied by our communal pots and pans. Ascetic practices all seem to mean saying no in order to say yes. A fast could clarify hunger, reify the nature of bread, give you the chance to thin the overgrown heart.

Every Wednesday my friend Jessica and I stuck only to hot tea, juices, and water, and we would pray. No coffee even. At work, I found an old nametag and wrote *Pray for Peace* on the back and pinned it earnestly to my shirt. I read up on Desmond Tutu, Mother Teresa, Elie Wiesel. I read up on the word itself, *fasting*, which comes from the idea of *holding fast*, as in *keeping* or *observing*. The Greek version translates *emptiness of food*; in Arabic it might have originally meant *to stand still*. People fast to atone or to dream dreams (like the Zulus of southeast Africa who know the continually stuffed body cannot see secret things); people fast before a sacrifice, before entering a sanctuary, after the first menstruation, before marriage, after a death. Muslims for Ramadan, Southern Baptists for the damned, a fast to ward off a plague of insects, a fast kept once the swarming locusts hit. I wonder if I did it because I relished the taste of my own renunciation—I have always wanted to know if you can love emptiness. I added a line from the poet Rilke to my copybook: *We can let ourselves be poor again*. I faxed a letter to President Bush. I puked up orange juice on one of the fasting days.

And on one of the days I scrambled two eggs and toasted bread and wrapped them up in foil to pass along to a guy who more or less lived in the bus stop on Irving Street on my way to work, because I'd read the Prophet Isaiah, Chapter 55: *Is it a fast that I have chosen, a day for a man to afflict his soul? Is it to bow down his head like a bulrush?...Is this not the fast that I have chosen: to loose the bonds of wickedness, to undo the heavy burdens, to let the oppressed go free? Is it not to share your bread with the hungry?* Robert was his name. I didn't ask Robert how he liked his eggs. He seemed to like the mushy sandwich, and I wished I could have a bite.

Weil used the word *gravity* to refer to our natural tendencies—doing all we can to get ours, looking out for number one. She urged that we seek the unnatural thing, that we renounce—look at and do not eat, do not take by violence into yourselves. Fasting is rehearsal for loving without devouring, but going without bread is not enough, there is another element in resisting gravity: feeding bread to another. She read everything. I'm sure she read Isaiah 55. And in this feeding act for her: *It is not surprising that a man who has bread should give a piece to someone who is starving. What is surprising is that he should be capable of doing so with so different a gesture from that with which we buy an object. Almsgiving when it is not supernatural is like a sort of purchase. It buys the sufferer.* How to properly give an egg sandwich? Supernaturally, or else it's a transaction. Weil's kind of giving is done through grace, of course, that's what she stressed, and grace—gravity's antonym—ultimately comes from outside of us.

But at twenty-two, and for the whole decade to follow in my life, everything was for me only a matter of my will. I do not know what the exchange meant to Robert. I was willing myself to love God and humankind. I thought this was something you could get right, even though Weil pressed on, relentless, with nuances I wouldn't begin to understand until later down the road: *He who gives bread to the famished sufferer for the love of God will not be thanked by Christ. He has already had his reward in this thought itself. Christ thanks those who do not know to whom they are giving food.*

At this desk now, with the wood wet, my body and eyes heavy, it feels strange to remember my younger, more fervent self. I think that Weil would see me—who I was then as much as now—as feral, undisciplined in thought, a cherry-picker of her ideas. She was not a systematic thinker but I am an even less systematic reader. The passages that make it into my copybook are often not the hard parts. After a while, I cannot sustain this line of thought and I crawl back into bed between sheets that need washing. I don't take ideas to their natural conclusion as she did, out there with migrant workers reciting the Lord's Prayer until the prayer and she became a single stab of light with dust motes. But I am hungry for some kind of bread, maybe my life lacks fervency. And my lover has left for the night and I wonder, when I miss him, what is it about him I miss? Just the food of him on my tongue? I feel there is a whole plane of loving I've yet to approach.

***

When I fell in love the first time, it was quick and irrevocable. Two weeks of knowing each other, then there were two years of letters—we were very good in letters—and then we were married with a corn roast at our wedding, and heirloom tomatoes and cousin John's side of beef cooked in a fire pit. With gladiola bouquets and rented tables set with cut flowers in mason jars—zinnias, Shasta daisies, poppies, cosmos, marigolds—the ceremony so sweet, outside on the grass. There was a slight unspoken hope in each of us—at least in me—for rain, so it wouldn't be so perfect. As though we wanted to stand separate from ourselves, not grasping at anything too tightly. *Beauty is a fruit which we look at without trying to seize it.* We each had our own Weil library. We were so careful. We preserved, I think, the rich and loamy loneliness in the other.

In one of his early letters, my would-be husband copied out excerpts from Weil's essay on friendship. He seemed already wary and, who knows, maybe he sensed the sad disaster to come and the big chunks of flesh we would eventually take out of each other. I did not marry a boy from home like Matthew of the hen-butchering days, though I'd always assumed I would. I married a philosopher who enclosed notecards with his letters with neat passages from Weil's essay: *Friendship is a miracle by which a person consents to view from a certain distance, and without coming any nearer, the very being who is necessary to him as food.*

I loved his idea, her idea, we had very good ideas. Embrace and not grasp, that is marriage, I thought. Intimacy doesn't have to mean violent possessiveness. We need not storm the door of the other's soul and body and gobble him up, take away his autonomy, get fat while he wastes away. The idea was to seek the other's good. But we lived too much in our ideas. We both wanted to be Weil, and the writer Dostoyevsky and the philosophers Wittgenstein and Buber and Levinas, instead of our clumsy selves. We wanted to live and breathe beautiful thought. But that is hard to do. I can close my eyes now and see us each as the naked hen body in my little-girl hands: I do not swipe either body down into a cow pie, frozen yet still filthy, but it takes so much effort to hoist them up for the whole trek, gravity pulling them down, the destroyed bodies headed into soups and covered dishes to be devoured, as husband, as wife, and the clear autumn sky above us all with the precise outline of leaves against that blue, like an incision.

To love purely is to consent to distance, it is to adore the distance between ourselves and that which we love. Yet in trying to preserve distance, you sometimes trip over your own carefulness. Sometimes the adoration of distance simply leaves you cold.

I don't know that we understood any of it, any of Weil's ideas, even the best ones. But how can you? All the contraries are true—for Simone: silence is sound, doubt is belief, absence is presence. And: *The beautiful is that which we desire without wishing to eat it.* We desire that it should be. We desire that his good fills its full space in all dimension in the center of the kitchen as he kneads and bakes bread and we watch him in his beauty from the other side of the room. But then we cross the room to taste because we cannot help it.

Perhaps we did devour one another in marriage, feed on each other. Perhaps we did not say, There is a beauty I do not eat, and I will give myself as meat instead, for my husband, for my wife.

Once, at a retreat cabin together in Michigan, we wondered what we could go without—not the red oil lamp, not the awful instant coffee, not the notebooks, not the colored pencils. Everything else could go. We lit the woodstove and talked softly in its simple light, then read quietly. We did not think we could live without each other. Some time later, did we really walk away and never meet again? Is that possible?

***

A few years ago, when still married, I gave a lecture on Simone Weil at the college in Oregon where I lived and taught. In the room was a doctor of systematic theology who was surprised the lecture was any good. So was I, but not for the same reason. He was surprised because he knew I was unsystematic; I was surprised because I was distracted by my marriage loudly falling apart. The falling-apart occupied the pre-lecture morning with heated argument, and also the post-lecture listless afternoon. But I knew, during the hour and a half with that room of students and faculty sitting in a circle, the points I wanted to focus on—the face of her I wanted to show, and there were many others I might have shown. I knew I wanted her version of love to mean something to them, even if it was an impossible version—or maybe because it was an impossible version. Simone had worked so hard to erase herself even as she wrote herself. The eraser always leaves a smudge and leaves someone trying to decipher what had been written there. We tried our best, the students and I.

In the lecture, I did not want to focus so much on renunciation, on not devouring, on willing yourself into ethical relation, on resisting gravity. I wanted to say something about grace—a concept I had never really understood in my bones—that thing out beyond our ideas and our attempts to make one thick cord out of our theory and praxis. In fact, it is grace that becomes real in the unraveling of such a cord. Grace bridges your deepest hunger to the deepest hunger in another. Then, you give bread out of hunger instead of saintliness, or surplus, you give with forgetfulness, beggar-to-beggar, not almsgiver-to-beggar. You give helplessly, and you love helplessly. It's as if, though you can't deny the gravity pulling at your small arms as you carry the hen bodies, you also sense some kind of hollowing-out of your bones that fills them with a lightness that lifts: you carry the burden, but it is somehow weightless.

Once, with my potter friend Nancy, my Oregon neighbor who has read nearly everything Weil ever wrote, I made a beggar bowl out of clay and she glazed and fired it for me to cup in my hands when I prayed, or when I did not know how to pray. To pray as a beggar made sense, to hold emptiness that way, even if I did not know how to love the emptiness. In time, Nancy wept with me about the marriage. And often, she and I both puzzled over the hardest part of Weil's eating metaphor, the weird part where God eats us.

In Weil's essay about beauty teaching us to love God, she writes: *The beauty of the world is the mouth of the labyrinth...if he does not lose courage, if he goes on walking, it is absolutely certain that he will finally arrive at the center of the labyrinth. And there God is waiting to eat him. Later he will go out again, but he will be changed, he will have become different, after being eaten and digested by God.* How forceful, how strange, Nancy and I always remarked, yet when I think about this part of Weil's metaphor now, it seems to me this is the way grace reaches the most stubborn of us: God eating us up as we stumble, hungry and thirsty, through the world, stubbornly doing our best with our belabored love, ready finally to be devoured, received, broken into morsels and fed out.

Ultimately, Weil thought God eats us like a mother bird and feeds others with our flesh. I can picture the bird feeding wide-mouthed babies in a nest caked with shit and mud, in their first few days of life on the outside, until they can handle a whole grub on their own. This bizarre process of grace, this being-eaten-by-God, is not what Weil accomplished by refusing food and dying of TB at age thirty-four, younger than I am now. I don't know what that accomplished. I know only that none of us fulfill our beautiful ideas in perfect gestures. That doesn't mean we should not have them. *Ideas come and settle in my mind by mistake,* she wrote in a letter to her friend Father Perrin. *Then, realizing their mistake, they absolutely insist on coming out. I do not know where they come from, or what they are worth, but, whatever the risk, I do not think I have the right to prevent this operation.*

The next morning, at this desk again, there is a stillness. I can hear the kindly mailman who limps. I can hear the rustling of the different selves in me, the girl with the peace pin—I like her, even though she's a fool—the girl hoisting carcasses and at other times folding fresh venison into freezer paper alongside one of her brothers and labeling it *tenderloin*, and at other times canning sausage and freezing corn, snapping beans on the porch into a bowl in preparation for the ordeal of supper—I like her too—the girl saying her marriage vows, trying to be a good wife, lecturing in a classroom and shaking—I am forgiving her. Such rustling seems louder these mornings in my thirties; it must be deafening at age eighty, like a pack of raccoons in your shed.

My mind wanders and I think about being a mother. I think of a little one feeding on and in me, a helpless little mite. I think of the world eating her as prey, then I picture her old, and myself too, feeble, someone spooning up applesauce to our lips. I wonder if Weil ever wanted to be a mother. Yes and no, no and yes, I assume. My girlfriends marry, buy houses, have their third child and offer their milk-full breasts. I wake in the middle of many nights ravenous. I want to fill notebooks. I do fill notebooks. I teach class and go to faculty meetings and squirm with my outcomes and assessments. I go to yoga and call my mother a few times a week and take food to my colleagues who forget to eat. I love a man, sometimes well, I try not to fear or be blind to this dangerous intimacy.

Probably she was pathological. Surely she was too austere. Not a life to follow. Or, at least, not a death to follow, the starving. But it seems to me that she lived her life feeding and being fed the real bread and meat, at times refusing it but, still, she was able to recognize it for what it was. *What is essential is to know that one is hungry...in the end we shall be fed and then we shall not believe but we shall know that there really is bread.* Hunger speaks to hunger, and says: Here is bread, you have never tasted bread like this. God, make me that kind of bread—consume me and feed my flesh to others—keep it all a secret from me, that is all right—take my notebooks, I am dying. It may have been her prayer. It may be mine.

Cattle Guard | *The Calf*

It happens on the stretch of road where everything happens, all of the significant events that fill childhood time to the brim. On this same stretch I ride the blue bike, fixed on my sister's back as she speeds before me on her yellow banana-seat cruiser past our neighbor's place—Mary Jane's—past the cattle guard at the mouth of her gravel drive, both of us aware that Mary Jane, a woman at Beatty Church, has the Holy Spirit deeply and soundly lodged within her, and today we have learned she has a brain tumor lodged the same. It's this road we cross with ice cream buckets to steal into the labyrinth of wild blackberry bushes where we get a whiff of a copperhead and bolt. It's here where my brother wrecks his racer into barbed wire and his long cut pusses up on his back with peroxide, and some thought of death breaks into my tiny invincible head with dread as absolute as his brave, pained whimper. And my other brother crosses this same eminent stretch of road to the field, with a mail-ordered Sears telescope that catches the moon for only a moment, since the moon, when brought down into our manageable universe and sucked into the telescope tube against the naked eye, becomes a fast mover. Even the event of God takes place on this road down which I walk the mile to Beatty Church in late summer, thumbing out one milkweed hull prematurely so the milk-wet silks stick to my arms, and another one more discerningly: it's dry to downiness, and my thumb threads through to set loose the fluff-seeds to propagate, and I get the notion that God is as intimate and touchable as the milkweed hull, infecting people like Mary Jane with visions and, I suppose, tumors, and giving way to my forceful thumb all the same. It is on this road that the calf gets caught in the cattle guard.

It happens like this: in the cold, I wear a snap-up rainbow vest, a boy's hat. The calf, a Guernsey heifer, is tied by its halter to the black pickup's hitch to be guided home, and I sit on the tire hump in the truck bed thinking it a perfect seat for me, the way children see everything held out just for them because they belong so deeply to their own lives. All four of us kids are in the truck bed, I the youngest. I feel the thrum-hum of tires slowly crossing the ridges of the cattle guard that is meant to keep cows from lumbering from the pasture into the road, but here we are crossing the trap with a calf pulled along behind us. The calf resists but is pulled forward and must step her tiny hooves into the ruts where she gets stuck and there is still the forward tug of the pickup. The rope goes taut, the truck keeps going, the calf's neck grows longer and I grow confused on the tire hump then distressed at the rigid rope and rigid neck and strained halter holding stubbornly, and the four of us scream to my father in the truck cab to stop—the calf's eyes going larger— surely he has forgotten about the cattle guard, thinking about all the other things that fathers think about when finally given some solitude. All breath sucks in and tension runs from calf flank up the spine to the elongated neck and wet pink velvet nose heaving, up to our open hands slapping the back window of the cab until he turns to see what all the racket is about.

That is all I can remember of this scene, where I sit now at my desk. Except I know the calf's leg does not splinter; alarm does not mature into horror, not on this day. But I don't know what does happen next, nor do I know what happened beforehand.

Maybe we'd bought the calf from Whitehair who owned the field surrounding Mary Jane's house, or maybe this was a calf of ours that had shimmied through the lax barbed wire fence and we were retrieving her. And maybe we were taking her to the barn to love on and bottle feed because weaning hadn't quite been accomplished, or taking her right to the butcher for winter veal, though at that time my mother told me we traded calves for meat and I believed her. Probably it was in fact one of Dolly's calves, and as my mother milked Dolly in the evenings I would have pressed my ear to the swollen bovine hide to listen to her pregnancy. And probably we got the calf home after the incident and tied her to the clothesline pole as we played wiffle ball, and we fed her ribey little apples from the tree in the yard. And surely, in time, she went to the butcher. But how did we get her out of that fix? Perhaps my father mercifully cut the tether, gathered the heifer in his arms, and carried her home. Perhaps my exasperated father did that and the calf acquiesced, went limp against his chest. But I don't know that that happened. The cattle guard scene exists as if held in a clear mushy globe, or sac, intact, with no before or after, and it exists as an image: a calf's breakable furry body pulled forward but she cannot go, resisting but she cannot go back, with her knobby legs caught in the ruts. Frozen like this in memory, the hot seizure of time and movement offers no way out. There is nowhere to go. It is a moment of impossibility, so it becomes for me—in the harsh bawling-out of the calf—a dramatization, or a tableau, of grieving.

I have both moved forward and moved back, literally. I lived in West Virginia for the first twenty-two years of my life, lived away for twelve years, and abruptly moved back—three years ago now, in the midst of divorce—to within an hour and a half drive of my childhood home. I was once again driving the curvy roads too fast with familiar ease, wondering, around each bend, if I might run into a younger, more whole version of myself. I took a tenure-track job with retirement and moved into a one-bedroom rental house I weekly get flowers for, I took up with a hound from the local shelter who claimed me, and I took some pleasure in being able to afford good cheese and good wine. But my interior state was bankrupt, everything was wrecked by the divorce, irreparable, and privately I dissolved daily into dry heaving. I missed my husband. I missed my life.

I remember one night, in the last month of our marriage, as my husband and I made our way east on the highway, unable to recognize our lives anymore or to name love or sadness or regret by their simple names, and I sat on a linoleum floor in a motel bathroom, under buzzing fluorescence, and it was cold, it was January—in Nevada, I think—with my husband becoming not my husband on the other side of the wall, shivering like a bird as if still outside and not in the cheap room, and I said to someone or something, Stop pulling—I cannot move. Everything felt too hot to touch, as if I were surrounded by glowing stove-burner coils and so could not budge, and as if I were engulfed in air that was somehow barbed when I breathed it but I had no choice but to breathe it. We could not find a way forward in marriage, nor could we return to what we had been. This seized-up feeling is likely familiar to any newly divorced person. There was no way out.

But of course, I do not write this on a motel bathroom floor. Somehow I got here, to this rented house, to this three-years-later self. And the movement baffles me.

Recently, I visited my parents who still live in the Whetsell Settlement house where I grew up. I walked my dog up that significant stretch of road and found mud and gravel filling the obsolete cattle guard ruts at the top of Mary Jane's drive, since the cows, and Mary Jane herself, are now long gone and someone grows corn in the fields there and had just harvested with a huge combine that had left the stalks all chewed and apocalyptic-looking. This spot once vast enough to hold all the volumes of my little life—such a rich storehouse of memory—was now strung with a useless fencerow and shrunken to a blip of rural landscape. I felt the constriction of time as well as its lording-over. Time regards no event or place worth stopping for. I had to get going. I had a lot of work to do for the new demanding job. I had an empty house waiting for me.

I write now about the calf because the image of liminality feels so accurate to grief. From the Latin, *limina* means threshold, the in-between place outside of the familiar but not yet inside a new possibility. The liminal place is the coarse rusted place, the desert, the scrub, the place that catches your little hooves in the cattle guard ruts and you are unable to go forward though you are pulled, and unable to return though you want more than anything else to do so. It is the place of exile from your life and is not a place we ever choose to go, though most of us will admit that going there teaches us what nothing else can and brings on a baptism into being human that cannot happen when we remain in control, riding our days with relative ease and success. Liminality is the crucible for a rough rebirth that involves relinquishing the aggregate gain of what you thought was hard-won knowledge and the security of your shored-up self. Until exile, I never questioned whether or not I loved my life because I'd never regarded it from the outside. Now, a permission is required to let myself love it; effort is required to let myself love it.

All spiritual traditions probably push us toward the threshold, the place of not-knowing. In my tradition, there is the biblical Noah, whom I can see frozen in that moment, unable to run out the ark's door last-minute, back to the world of the damned he was born to, and also unable, in that moment, to turn toward a God whose floodwater would fill the lungs of every baby field mouse that wasn't one of the two on the ark of salvation—the impossible moment of envisioning the mice-babies paddling for the sky, God looking on, their paws the size of matchstick heads, until the black water would drown them while Noah would be safe, afloat. Or Lot's wife from later in the Book of Genesis, fleeing the cursed city of Sodom—but then frozen, unable to return to the life she knew, but unable to follow her husband up the hill to safety. It's a liminal moment of grieving—for a microsecond or an eternity—before she turns, somehow chooses to turn and look back, knowing the consequences, and her skin crystallizes to salt, maybe her lungs metamorphosing first, or her eyes, her heart. The kernel of these stories burns brightly with the moment of change and loss of everything, the moment that forges the soul in fire. And liminality can stretch to forty years in the desert for the wandering ex-slaves; it can be downright interminable for Job with his sense of self peeling off painfully with each layer of his leprous skin. And it seems to me that, contrary to the sermonizing of these stories, they do not reveal lessons easy to articulate.

I also write about the calf because I am not there now, at the threshold, though I cannot say that I am on the other side of it either since that suggests linearity that doesn't feel quite right. And my own grief space of divorce was far from Job-like in its proportions, but it is the measure of liminality that I know and can try to describe. I am not there now, I am elsewhere, and I have learned things I can't coherently express, and I am different in ways that are difficult to gauge. I can move and breathe now, I have even fallen in love again, though differently—I'm more gun-shy, less enmeshed—the embrace feels wondrous though sometimes foreign, the way joy after disappointment is not exactly what it was in its first, native form. I have a more present-tense life now, less of the reflective impulse that I used to have probably as a result of an old-fashioned childhood with a milk cow instead of a Sega Genesis or dial-up internet. And also less of a planning impulse. I used to list goals for the year that would produce, I felt, the kind of person I desired to be, someone who would go to Greece before age thirty, would learn banjo and not something boring like piano, would garden in raised beds—lists written with careful casual messiness and stuck on the fridge to remind me of how to achieve a life that would be approved of, applauded. My husband was part of this; we mutually imagined ourselves into some wildly beautiful people. And on a list more private I wrote the goal of a baby and how we would leave Oregon where we lived most of our married life and move to West Virginia and the baby would become a little girl on a blue bike, in a little dress flapping, some streamers from the handlebars rippling as she'd ride up that stretch of road past the cattle guard to meet my mother, lilacs infusing the air everyplace around them both with a damp scent, and the girl, my girl, would exist in that contained bowl of a world that I was once held by. Anyway, then there was the divorce, and so the question of a child, along with the other items on the long list, moved someplace out of my reach.

There are other differences. People seem less knowable, more fractured. So does God. I worry sometimes that connections, when fully exposed, can only be superficial and selfish, and freedom in unmarriedness only isolating. I worry that cleverness is replacing wisdom in what I read because I struggle to believe in wisdom, collegiality replacing friendship because I jettisoned many old friendships that seemed to belong to a different self, mild appetite replacing hunger because hunger is too frightening in its insatiability, and reason or practicality replacing blind faith because I don't feel blind. And there is the strange forgetting, too: the way you begin to forget the textures of your marriage so that the first time it snows in your new life and the world goes white you sense that the same quietly disastrous thing is happening to your memory and you hope maybe that means you're not as shallow and strange as you fear because snow only conceals, does not obliterate—surely somewhere the intensity of relation and connection still resides in you even though your days sometimes have a pallor, a vagueness.

Some stay at that threshold an awfully long time, like my friend whose father has Alzheimer's and cries each time she leaves him, like those living with abuse, with chronic pain, with the threat of beheading or torture or paralysis. Some lives are indeed Book-of-Job-like. People bear all sorts of unbearable things. I know I am fortunate to have gone to a place that felt impossible only once in my life so far—that place of alarm and estrangement from the self.

Some end the painful liminal hovering by suicide. But for most of us, the moving on with life is predictable; most people don't stay there, perhaps just because of tiredness and time—give it a year, they all said to me, because most of them knew, most of them had had such a year themselves. Who knows what pulls us out of it? It could be neglect, or forgiveness. I read in a self-help book that forgiveness means seeing the childhood hurts that have hardened someone, seeing the panorama of the person and not just the fuckup. And maybe it did help me to see my husband as a kid napping or on his bike, and seeing myself too, also as more than a fuckup, as an open-hearted little girl belonging to her life.

Maybe it was God's Spirit, God's hand that pulled me out—some would say so. That image of my father possibly enfolding the heifer in his arms and lifting her out of her predicament, that's a nice image. But the truth is I can't say why I'm not there, any more definitively than I can say how we freed the Guernsey heifer from the iron ruts without her leg splintering.

After awhile you just become a divorced person, and the odor of tragedy fades from your life. Friends don't sniff at it every time they call, the wound of holidays and anniversaries and memory-infused objects goes unremarked, wedding-gift kitchen appliances become practical, your family plans Christmas. People expect things of you again—to chip in on your cousin's baby shower gift, to render the spiritual gleanings from divorce into comprehensible lessons of God's comfort and faithfulness. Your girlfriends announce their engagements and discuss their wedding plans without furtively checking your face for how you're taking it. You become a thirty-five-year-old academic with a dog but no children, newly cognizant, when you lift your head from grading essays, that your mother, now married for forty-plus years, had four children by the time she was your age.

How we get from there to here is maybe not the interesting thing.

The interesting thing is the nostalgia for the heartache. How you miss it.

How, when you study that image of the calf caught in the cattle guard, you see the alarm in her eyes, yes, but also the surprise felt in finding her body in such a state, finding that she in fact has no control, she is merely here in brilliant pain that clarifies she is alive. For me, in that liminal state, a kind of chemical change transmuted my striving and my conscious self-shaping and my perfectionism into breakage, and the whole pulsing ache was the most honest prayer I've ever been able to pray. At the threshold, I had for the first time a sharp sense of being somehow loved in the midst of failure. Then, after a time, you're not there anymore. You begin to know yourself after the event of estrangement—responsible and capable again, you can meet deadlines, you can have a relationship with a man again, in real friendship, you are not ruined for intimacy. You can shop for your own groceries and eat meals again like a normal person because life has become possible and level. You are relieved it's all over, you are content even. So you have difficulty understanding why on earth, at an unguarded moment, you grow suddenly desperate for that bright pain to return. You cannot understand why you miss the astringent air, why you long for the harsh naked bawling to come from your animal throat.

Resurrection | *The Boy in the Blue Sweatshirt*

I recall the face of a boy wearing a blue sweatshirt, and I want to tell him that I've fallen in love and that I saw a fox midday like a flare, that I saw a black bear in the laurel just this evening and that the roar of life astounds me. And I want to describe the way a lover stands on the stoop, smoking a cigarette that he's rolled with borrowed papers, waiting for her to pull up in the car, and the way he will say nothing in particular to her, and then enfold her. I have things to tell this boy in a blue hooded sweatshirt, and he has things to tell me. When I look at the boy's face through the lens of memory, I feel as though it is the first day of my life and I want it to be the first day of his.

I met the boy at a week-long summer camp in late July, the summer before I started high school. But I didn't meet him in person. He was the star of a film shown to us by the Kentucky Mountain Bible College group from Asbury. They showed it in the chapel on the last day of church camp—I don't remember the name of the boy or the name of the film. It had a Seventies luster and the boy had dark hair and dark eyes. The film flickered up from a clacking projector onto a white screen that they'd pulled down over the wall-size Jesus, painted there as a shepherd with a flock of adoring sheep gathered at the hem of his white robe. I remember only one clip of the film: the boy was shivering in his sweatshirt as he walked toward a plane on a runway. The plane appeared full and ready for takeoff but it was waiting on him. Behind him a little ways, his family stood crying, not wanting him to go. I didn't see the boy's face for some time, only the faces of his family, especially his mother, as she reached toward her son but was held back by some men who remain vague in my mind. The voiceover told us that the boy was about to leave his family behind for good—the boy knew Jesus, but his family didn't because he'd never shared the Gospel message with them, and now he was leaving them for heaven because it was time. And we kids sat on the edge of our chapel pews as the boy kept walking, but when he reached the steps to board the plane, he stopped and turned, and we saw his face.

He looked, then, like a boy I would maybe want to go swimming with. He looked reckless and hurt. His eyes stayed locked with his mom's until he finally boarded. None of us campers had ever been on a plane, but we could feel it take off and we were each ripped in two. After the film, though we couldn't explain it really, we were all caught up in tears and making promises, listing names in our ocean-scene journals: *Christie, Summer, Aunt Kathy, Eric*, we'd make sure we'd tell them the Gospel about Jesus. The filmmakers and the Asbury group had succeeded to some degree, emboldening us into missionaries, into those who would recruit for the next world though our feet were barely wet with this one.

I wasn't clear about the symbolism of the plane (nor am I now)—I was uncertain whether the boy was supposed to be dying and then going to heaven on the plane, or whether it was the Second Coming of Christ and all that, a time of last chances when every man, woman, and child would stand at the threshold of eternity and be judged. What did clearly register with me, then and now, was the departure of the boy from this world, and the fact that the departure was somehow caused by belief in resurrection, in Jesus's defeat of death and sin on the cross, and the resulting gift of eternal life. But what has remained most vivid in my memory is the boy's face.

What is it the boy wanted? The mysterious thing about an illustration like this film is that, in tugging at our imaginations for the purpose of teaching us a doctrine, the illustration still takes on a life of its own in each mind, in whatever way each peculiar imagination plays within it. So, as a young girl of fourteen—though I did realize that the film's voiceover was chastising the black-haired boy as a warning to us, was saying that he had essentially failed in his great calling to bring his family into the fold of sheep who huddle at Jesus's garment hem, and was admonishing us to do better—though I realized this, what I saw on the boy's face was resistance to the leaving, and my imagination stole away with this resistance.

In his face I saw love for his mother, yes, but also more: I saw the sting of a baseball caught barehanded, a mitt lent to a smaller kid; in his eyes I saw a study of his hand on his knee beside a shy girl's hand on her knee; I judged that the boy's hair had not been washed and so he was not prepared to go anywhere and didn't want to go; I felt that he was about my age, a year older maybe, like a brother; I understood that he had started to see himself as beautiful, no longer reserving such a word for only the girls he'd wave to, but finding deep water in his own dark eyes, and he wondered about whose image he was made in. And then I surmised that he was not leaving at all, but he was being taken—feet light and unplanted—and new compounded fears struck me. This was a camp for mostly poor kids, and I suppose I was relatively poor, by some standards, and I was better prepared for the afterlife than I was for starting high school in the fall, with my canvas shoes and hand-me-down jeans. But at the thought of being taken like the boy in blue, away on a jet plane, for good, I was newly afraid of losing the small life I was living. I was afraid of failing in my duties. I was afraid, most of all, of my own resistance to going when the time came.

It's true that the scene of departure in the film inspired a missionary spirit in us, somewhat, but it also moved us to these fears and to mourning—that is to say, it was the last day of our week together and we sat in the chapel at Aldersgate Camp in Cranesville, just a few miles out of Terra Alta where we had watched the Independence Day parade a few weeks earlier, and this chapel was lit like a lonely wick in the palpable dark of the West Virginia mountains. And it was a day among the first days of our chance at living, and we wanted no part of a resurrected afterlife just yet. We wanted to smack up fresh against this world first, though we had no words for that. We had only the words of hymns by John and Charles Wesley and the praise choruses taught to us by the awkward Asbury group and the Hedrick sisters who shared the stage with them. And we had the King James Bible, we had the verses which we engraved on wood with wood burners and carved with rotary tools. It would take us a long time to get our own words for it. Maybe that's what I'm still doing here as I sit and peer for a time at this boy in blue, his dark hair mussed and his face frozen in my memory. I try to see him more clearly in this present good mixture of light and rain today, to say what can be said about our young lives on that last day, and what might be said, too, about resurrection.

I loved Aldersgate Evangelical Camp. I started going the summer I was eight years old, first to Primary Camp, then to Intermediate the next few summers, then finally to Senior Camp, the week reserved for middle school and high school kids. On the last day of a week of camp, we came out clinging to each other, regarding one another with a felt weight of importance—farm kids mostly, who gulped back some fear in the face of the big world and in the more immediate faces of town kids in Kingwood who would be our schoolmates in the fall.

On the last night, a younger one among us at the campfire ring looked up and asked, Will my heart turn black again? And an older one, a junior counselor, said nothing, just put an arm around the younger one, not sure how long the heart can stay clean (it was something she would pray over). Then the fear of the blackness washed over the counselor and made her hold the younger with both arms, both their faces lit up by flames. And the chill was starting to drift down; it could have almost frosted since Cranesville is so high in the mountains; the nights in late July could get that cold. Everyone had on a sweatshirt or tied one round his waist on the way to the campfire ring. And it was a solid darkness at the camp, with one far-reaching light up near the dining hall (though it was not far-reaching enough because many of us tripped in the dark going to the bathhouse at night) and there were also the tiny porch lights at the front doors of the cabins, but they couldn't reach down to the campfire ring either. The darkness swallowed us. And in the Bible, there was a verse in the fifth chapter of Paul's second letter to the Corinthians which I pondered later for its mystery and its evocation of those dark mountains: *For we who are in this tent groan, being burdened, not because we want to be unclothed, but further clothed, that mortality may be swallowed up by life.* Bible scholars have said Paul meant that we suffer in this mortal body, this tent, but, even so, we do not long to be disembodied but to have a resurrected body which God will give us—as though that explains it. The flames of the campfire ring, the consuming fire with its spark-ash flakes that spit upwards, was all the light we had, except for the few small flashlights we had brought. But that was at the very end of the day. Much came before that.

It cost us each five dollars for a week at camp in Cranesville. There were two cabins, the boys' cabin large enough to house some classrooms, the girls' cabin with its drop-ceiling left unfinished: one large room with the beams still bare so we girls could swing from bunk to bunk. The camp had a standing odor of wet towels, mildewy from being crumpled in the corner by a camper late for breakfast line-up when, even as older kids, we put our noses into the wet-haired head in line in front of us. The tribe with the straightest line got to go first into the dining hall of long tables with folding chairs. Corile Wilhelm—wife to Reverend Berlin Wilhelm who ran the camp—had the bowls of oatmeal and the plates of toast ready for us in the center of the tables, the same number of pieces of toast as there were chairs.

I lined up behind Clarissa, and early in the week I tried to determine her shampoo, Pert Plus or Prell, its scent masked by the moldy smell that comes from using the same towel too many times. But late in the week the bath house reservoir ran dry and towels stayed crumpled like shed snakeskins, or bodies after the rapture of the saints. Most of us, including me, weren't yet in high school, but those who were went in the car with Paige up the road to a parsonage where they could wash.

Some girls wore bandanas. I wore my unwashed hair in a low pony tail, and a blond boy named Jason Skipper flicked it as he lined up behind me. He put his toes right up against my heels and made me feel warm, and I stood that way on the morning of the last day, nosing my way into Clarissa's long dirty braid in front of me.

Classes in the rooms of the boys' cabin lasted the rest of the morning until tribal meeting. Though we were a bit old for it, one of the counselors from the Bible college in Asbury led my class in a craft with half-burnt matches. Most of us glued together a cross with no Christ. We studied the Book of Revelation, the twelve foundations of heaven laid for each of the twelve disciples, each one a precious stone: *jasper, sapphire, emerald, sardonyx, sardius, beryl, topaz,* and so on. All of us girls, but few boys, wrote the names of the stones down in our journals with oceans on their covers, or lilies, or kittens with bubble letters crooning *Purrfect.*

I thought the Asbury counselor was pretty, with a face much smoother than mine with its random acne. But I remember her acting too old for her lovely young face, in her long matronly skirt and no earrings. She seemed to have passed from childhood straight to old age, and as I think of her now, I think of the part of her that had been lost in that passage. I was, at fourteen, getting ready to leave my child body which I knew to be as mighty and obstinate and unsupple as a hardwood. But I did not want to leave it behind in exchange for a body hidden by a matronly skirt. The tug was toward something else, something that was veiled for me then, but it had to do with the way I swelled up with heat when Jason Skipper stood near. And even at fourteen, even then, maybe that tug also got me considering a new meaning of the resurrection that was preached to us, since resurrection seemed to involve leaving a place behind, a place you may or may not have come to love.

Just before lunch line-up, we assembled in the chapel that had a cement floor and narrow green pews designed for bodies even smaller than ours. A white podium stood at the front, before the wall-size acrylic Jesus among his flock. Lois Hedrick and the Asbury singers led us a cappella or with guitar, often in a round, groups divided according to which tribe we were in—Joseph, Benjamin, Reuben, or Judah, named for the sons of Jacob.

On the last day, I arrived early for music with Autumn, Clarissa's sister, and she told me that she and Ben Grose would be writing letters to one another after camp. That painting of Jesus loomed before us as she giggled, but his eyes weren't watching over us, as eyes in a wall painting often do. In fact, Christ seemed much too preoccupied with the sheep to fool with us. I wanted to share some news of my own with Autumn, and I considered sharing about my matchstick cross-with-no-Christ that I'd made that morning, since she had been in a different craft class. But that wasn't as compelling, so I inquired further into how Ben had asked for her address. He'd asked after their tribal meeting in the woods—they were both in the tribe of Reuben—with his hands in his pockets, the way all the Grose boys stood while they talked, sons of a potato farmer.

I sit and consider the matchstick cross now, as well as the huge acrylic Jesus on the chapel wall, and I consider how the painters hadn't depicted him raised-up or crowned. They hadn't painted the slit where his feet had disappeared up through the clouds, but they'd painted him against a backdrop of cheesy-green pasture grass, among sheep, dressed in a silly white bedsheet-tunic, with his hands pushed out to the touchable world of briars and lamb snouts, wet and steamy most likely. Still, people called him the Risen Lord, the Resurrected. He was with God, they said, among the angels, from the beginning, and then up there again in that throne at the end, but what interrupted that enthroned state was a passage through here. Passing over grass and gravel places with their soft and hard surfaces, and touching them.

What to make of it? And why make anything of it at all? Why give it so many words here when there are plenty of other topics to explore and tasks to finish? I suppose because of the roar of life and the inevitable emptiness that answers back to it from the grave. And maybe because I feel a strange grief sometimes only from sitting close to someone I love, like I did last Sunday in a church, our bodies flush in a pew. Because throughout the hymn we were singing—the sturdy measures of Blessed Assurance—a shriveled older woman peered at my face blankly from her choir seat up front.

As I study on it, the resurrection seems to involve more than going to heaven when you die, transported like a jet passenger. I do believe in it, make of that what you will. But I do. I've seen too many fearless faces not to. Yet I am not sure how something like the resurrection takes effect, how it might swallow you up in its life while you sting with youth and while you live in mortal cracking bones. But I imagine it sometimes, like: you look at your life and see it as the paltry thing that it is and then you lean back into it, as a kid leans into a bed of moss, and you're freed from something, you claim nothing, you leave no trace, you are only left with a trace of everything, you have memorized nameless birds' underbellies, you are no longer a martyr or a crusader or anyone of much importance, just a bum with a hammer, fixing loose railings now and then.

Or like: you are in love, and you feel it in body, though your body, like many others, is blasted, your feet swollen with bad cholesterol. There will be a time when you will break apart and unenlist yourself from the world, you'll quit the urge to yelp with rage at a low branch snagging locks of hair loose from tidy clips (you'll not mind the mess, the need for prettiness burning less hotly in your blood), you'll quit calling from the kitchen, quit limping from the bed. Your lover will call for you at the first light of morning, missing you, filled up with you like a deep well with water, and the fullness will contain sadness but also much more than sadness.

But I didn't think on these things then. I wondered instead, as the other campers trickled in, and then Lois and the Asbury folks with their song sheets, what Ben and Autumn would write to each other, how they would even begin their letters and how they would end them and whether they'd be able to say it all in between. Would they struggle to find words to talk about how they loved Aldersgate, how we all loved it—even with the strictness of the counselors and the way they could make us feel so scared and ashamed—how it has given us riches, scarred and chipped ones, but riches all the same?

Or would the two grow out of it and grow more interested in cars and in the brand names of jeans and in making something of themselves?

After lunch, there was a way in which the last day mounted to softball and kickball and then descended into quiet hour when we each lay in our bunks and prayed or braided our dirty hair or thought about the way one of the boys brushed by us at second base. We turned reflective, and we turned our faces toward evening, almost reverently, so to be sure to remember it.

Besides Ben Grose, Jason Skipper was the boy whom all the girls loved and whom, on the last day, only Sarah got. There were signs of her claim on him in the middle of the week when she tied his sweatshirt round her waist, wore it when it rained (the rain filled the reservoir a bit and so a few of us got to wash in the bath house; I was one of the few, and afterward I added a smear from Crystal's bottle of *Beautiful* because I thought nothing in the world smelled as good as that perfume, and I hoped Jason would agree).

There was a slate-rock stage beside the fence that divided the camp from a field that grazed someone's cattle, and here we had our vespers before supper, led by each tribe in its turn, near sundown, toward the hillside where the other campers sat, some sitting close to one another. That summer I was in the tribe of Benjamin and that evening, though some of us may have been too old for it, I led us in a song with hand motions.

Most of the songs were the same from year to year, from Intermediate into Senior Camp, with a few new ones thrown in by the Asbury team. Perhaps, intentionally or not, they kept the songs the same so to keep us young and childish. Maybe they knew how difficult living would be for us in time. They wished to keep us from the sadness. They knew that someday the world would deliver an unbelievable grief. In many ways, we were about to start life, with its abiding shadow of death, with its sadness. And I wanted it. I want it still. But how to tell them, through the songs and the handclaps, that we wanted the sadness?

After the last line-up and a supper of raviolis and white bread, we all dressed up for the evening chapel service. Back in the girls' cabin, Paige stopped me with my hand on the screen door latch because I'd put on a loose-fitting white sweater over top of my dress. She was a kind older counselor who seemed different from women like Corile or the Asbury singers. The homemade dress I wore had capped sleeves and a fitted bodice, yoked at the waist. It was pretty with pastels, like an Easter dress. Paige saw me pull the baggy cardigan sweater close to me and said I didn't have to cover up as though I didn't want to look like a woman. I felt the dress on my skin, on my body, I'd washed before the reservoir had emptied again. I blushed at her but I slid the sweater off my shoulders and cradled it in a rumpled ball with my jean purse, and I pushed the screen door latch open.

There was a missionary who had come with the Asbury group and he gave the chapel message without notes. Since it was the last night of camp, each of us girls had a cheap camera in a purse along with the lily- or kitten-cover journal. The missionary talked about his year in Africa, in Guinea-Bissau, and the way most of the missionaries got sick when they used an outhouse for the first time but how he, being from a poor farm town, was well-acquainted with that kind of toilet and could connect with the people in that regard, and he got some laughs since we were all familiar with outhouses, too, and could start to imagine ourselves with the African tribe, trying on a long bead necklace like the one the missionary wore over his tie. He spoke as though he'd memorized the words, wielding his right hand like a blade as he spoke. He broke into a sweat, despite the cool Cranesville night air, as he crescendoed to the altar call, a call to a life lived by the power of the resurrection, by the power of the resurrection of the Lord. He asked us to surrender everything to Jesus, and he asked Lois, Can we sing four-oh-six, "I Surrender All"? She led us with her watery voice, and we followed, many of us without needing to open the hymnal.

It was then, after this closing song, that the Asbury members (who were caught up as we all were) pulled down the white screen over Jesus's acrylic face and shut off the overhead lights and started the film that featured the boy in the blue sweatshirt. And it was then—with the musky scent of Jason Skipper tugging at me from two rows up—that I met the boy in blue and glimpsed in his face all that which I was unable to give words to. The day had been so full that, when I met the sudden resistance in him, my eyes stung.

He had been a poor disciple of the Gospel, but I knew the boy had done the best he could. And though I was meant to see a rejection of this world in his face as he turned—a complete surrendering of it—I saw what I saw: a rejection of an otherworldliness. I felt strangely proud of him, comradely and sisterly, proud that he would not board the plane without looking back to show in his face something beyond the thin illustration that the film posed: a secret pact between him and me, with him glowing before he left, in the way that we can glow from even a mishandled fire, with him assuring me that the resurrection meant more than simply being taken. I only wanted him to stay so that we could work out our own words for the resurrection by practicing them as the world would change thereafter and as we would grow older and would move about in that world, soaked with its wet like white shirts in harsh bleach-water. The boy knew more about resurrection power than the filmmakers did, more than the missionary, more than any of us in that chapel, at least in the way I imagined him then.

I consider the boy's glowing face now, and something of that secret pact remains. And I imagine resurrection again, like: you spit up blood into paper towels and the doctors aren't sure why, and that's only part of what the years have given you, so you think, sure, you would love to come back in a brilliant new body—maybe, and maybe you will desire that even more fervently when the life roar becomes more and more muffled—but what is most remarkable to you, even apart from the new body, is this thing that allows you to forgive your present body, to forgive your bitterness and forgive the dailiness of dying and your daily participation in it.

The Hedricks and the Asbury folks who wanted to protect us—and themselves—did so by trying to contain mystery within the walls of a tiny chapel surrounded by all that darkness. But some of us would start high school that next month, so maybe it was such that we in our limber bodies—which knew well a piece of land, the rise of the road, the path of a fox or a four-wheeler or, in the case of Ben and Autumn, a warm press of the hand—we would need to know how to live in the whorls of mystery outside of those walls, in the dark. To know a daily resurrection in the midst of things, through embarrassment or pain or disappointment, and not simply after it all passes—might this belief not have ached within the boy in blue?

But the film caught us up that night, and we listed the names of those to whom we'd tell its message, and since it was the last night of camp we dried our eyes and turned to the next page in our beloved journals to record each other's addresses, promising to write late into the fall and winter. The film had started some of the boys talking again about what do to if the Second Coming of Christ happened while we were still living (we even worried it would be soon); they made arrangements for where to meet during the great tribulation times. We'd meet at the camp, they said, and we'd call it the Afterglow since the darkness all around us would be great. The Battle of Armageddon would be stirring up before or after the rapture. We didn't know. These were words from our studies of the Book of Revelation; they were words still without shape or shading in our minds. After the weight of the departure of the boy in the film, we were grateful for our own distracting fascination with the rapture. The idea of it gathered us up in a cloud that would soon enough deposit us back down on the mountain ground, as kids stung by the world as it was, by the days growing colder and by the beginning of high school. But first, there was the campfire ring down the hill from the chapel, and on the last night, some of us walked down there with flashlights and some without, and those without held onto another's sweatshirt sleeve.

A Good Day | *My Mother*

Love, how the hours accumulate. Uncountable.
The trees grow tall, some people walk away
and diminish forever.
The damp pewter days slip around without warning
and we cross over one year and one year.

       —Li-Young Lee, "Braiding"

Morning

My mother's hands are older than she is, and as rough as the worn burrs she works loose from the dog's fur. It is morning. A string of Christmas lights dangles from the doorframe in a lopsided U, her task interrupted by the dog's collapse on the porch. Mom has made a straw bed in the barn and, over the past few days, has carried the dog to the bed, like an infant with legs and arms curled limp from a day's play. Glossy black fur gone gray, rust-colored tufts around the teats. But the dog crawled back to the porch. Now Mom hurries to put a bucket of water beside the bed of straw in the barn and comes back to scoop up the dog. It goes slack. Just dies right there in her arms, on the path midway between the house and barn door, on the path she's worn into the ground carrying feed buckets and egg baskets and pails of cinders. She strokes the dead dog, snags a burr; she lays the furry body in the straw bed and tries to pet it back to life.

  Nothing has ever died in her arms before. There was the calf stillborn in the pasture, but she watched from a window in the house. She recalls the Scripture, *He breathed his last*, and thinks, *Now I know what that looks like.* She's not one to speak tenderly of animals, hollering often at the whitetail deer that munch her lettuce; she's butchered hens with no remorse; she once shot a groundhog with a twelve-gauge. Even so. She has felt, freshly, death's interruption, and now this dog has interrupted her hanging of the twinkle lights on a day with a dead wind. Her father-in-law C.S. has died, after she and Dad took him in for five months, after she became so sensitive to his movements that she would smooth the wrinkles from the rugs where he walked.

Death separates, Mom writes in her letter to my brothers and sisters and me that morning—*it just seems like there's been a good bit of it*. And then, further down on the loose leaf: *when the life breath goes out— absent from the body, present with the Lord.*

It is morning where I am, too, several states west of her. I have hung my laundry and put on lotion, trying to trick my hands into not being like my mother's. I'm thirty-one, as old as she was when she birthed me. As yet, I am childless, birthing only manuscripts. I get going on my deskwork. This morning, I will write about her, about her days and the way they have shaped my own, these days that slip, however shaped, through our fingers.

She prefers the dawn. She wakes before five and tugs a ratty black sweater over her nightgown, reads the Bible, then dresses and pulls on her Tingley boots. She heads to the garden before the sun can burn off the fog, but she stops at the door, goes under the dome of stove light to start a letter on a paper scrap, only a paragraph before she remembers the hot sun rising and quits the letter mid-sentence for the door.

She takes walks down Wilson Hill and back, toting her prayer list of names: mostly those dying of cancer, but also my siblings and me and our crises; also the Albright foster sisters who were just split up; also the President and the War. But sometimes, in her rush of uphill movement, she simply gives a bit of thanks with no room for anything else during the fifty-minute walk.

Some pray the hours; Mom prays the minutes—I am a little girl sticking my head out the back screen door; Aunt Kathy is on the phone and I holler for Mom, but she's talking loudly to someone else, scraping the chicken manure off her Tingleys. *Who are you talking to?—Just God*—and how irritated she sounds, the conversation unfinished, or, perhaps, weighted on one side. She leaves off, mid-sentence, grabbing the receiver—*Kathy?*

Before his death, C.S. sleeps in the hospital bed in the living room. Mom still wakes early, reads Psalms at the table within earshot of his breathing. He is a small man-comma curved under the sheets, his oxygen machine a heavy whisper. With his presence in the house, she dresses in the bathroom and sees how very small her eyes are in the mirror, but they enlarge by and by; she picks up Dove soap for her face, cheap lipstick to rouge her cheeks.

C.S. dies, and that morning, she has a hair appointment—*do I go?* She doesn't know.

And her hair—she touches it, apologizes always for its mess and its lack of shape, but then she threads her fingers through it with secret pleasure, for she's never wanted hair she could pick out of a catalogue. She thinks things are clearer when your hair begs a dollop of styling gel, just as they're clearer when you've got under twenty dollars in a checkbook and even less in a wallet but your jeans are nice and snug, line-dried, and the fall air chills your hands till they sting red with the work you have to do today. She throws herself full force into work, alongside Dad: burning brush, covering the chicken house windows with plastic for the winter, liming the garden, ousting the new potatoes. But doing the work is not for the purpose of arriving, finished, ready for a prize and a rose-pinning. It's immersion. It's work that's meant to create a place inside the day for others to come into—come evening—to sit. And that evening light, radiating from the hues of the work itself, will slant onto the porch where the others will sit, and their faces will glow pink and gorgeous.

A day, a life, is not a means to an end. What do I think is urgent for her today? That we do not, will not, die alone.

I get up from my desk and fiddle with the coffee grinder till it cooperates. *It is necessary for me,* Thomas Merton says to me from the note card taped to my wall, *to see the first point of light which begins to be dawn. It is necessary to be present alone at the resurrection of Day, in the blank silence when the sun appears. In this completely neutral instant I receive from the Eastern woods, the tall oaks, the one word 'DAY,' which is never the same. It is never spoken in any known language.*

The morning light in here ignites the sill so that even the upturned Japanese beetle carcasses look radiant. As the days slip past, how are we to know if they are good days? How to know a path, my own path, like my mother's between the back screen door and the barn, etched by her years of footfalls into the parted fescue grass?

Noon

Mom naps a noon hour of my girlhood—what a rarity—and I lie with her on the bed. I'm lucky to be beside her with no dad around, no older siblings. I see her with her glasses off: a pretty, naked face with lipstick on her lips, her cheeks and chin dabbed with the tip of the same tube of lipstick and rubbed in. She will not spend the money for the compact with a mirror, icing-pink blush with a soft cosmetic brush. Wet with sweat, her short brown curls sweep up from her forehead and don't pester her. I realize, maybe for the first time, that she exists apart from me, a woman much more powerful and more fragile than I can comprehend. Her eyes are not scrunched, as they sometimes are, with her suspicions so various: suspicion of "implants," the back-to-the-earth hippies who move to rural West Virginia with, she thinks, some sort of agenda; suspicion of any agenda, of crisp computer-printed bulletins in churches with their *Order of Worship*; suspicion of the false note in a sermon when the preacher's voice goes shrill then soft, like a fickle radio station, and of the common-law marriage, of versions of the Bible newer than the King James, of any woman preacher, of religious robes, symbolic icons, feminists, sad foreign films and their tedious subtitles, of self-help books, prayer manuals. Of any claims that have no clout for her once the morning fog burns off and what's left is the day's work.

On the bed, her eyelids are closed like pale, veiny curtains. She must see in her dreams a vision of fire, or of a workless day, or of the dress she lost in a basement flood, her wedding dress with a wide-brimmed hat to match.

Then it is autumn, after twenty autumns have passed; it's a warm spell, so one afternoon she takes her ironing board out to the porch since C.S. likes to sit out there in an easy chair. She plugs the iron into a long extension cord and progresses from simple pillowcases to jeans to blouses with tricky pleats. Nasturtiums trail from her hanging baskets to the porch floor. The hen that escapes the coop each day, with little reprimand, perches on the arm of the porch swing while C.S. chatters like a magpie about his days as county sheriff and about what he'd like for supper. She forgets that the pink blouse she irons will one day dissolve to dust—or else she lives so completely in that knowledge that it makes her love the blouse all the more. What makes us love something? Maybe its finitude. Or our blithe, present forgetfulness.

Mom irons till dusk. It is one of those days when a person is in love with her life because she is still getting to know it—she later cleans up his diarrhea that gets all over the piano bench and bed sheets and living room floor—and she's still getting to know it.

At my desk, it is almost three p.m. now, a terribly beautiful three p.m., and I wish it were raining. Then, suddenly, with a humid swell, it is. The rain starts, and, like a fool, I leave my laundry hanging; I keep writing. The rain slows me. It gives permission for more deskwork.

My mother, too, though she propels herself always, forward flung and forceful (she shoots the moon in cards, always overbids her hand—bids three on the Ace of Spades alone—overapologizes, overbudgets a trip, overdoes the spread of pork chops and a batch of rolls on the table; underspends only on her underwear and shoes), she loves the rain. When it rains, there is pause, the catching of breath, a permission announced by the hard sure bullets on the tin roof. Permission for her letters. She pulls out the letter that she began in the morning, before the day's work, and she resumes.

Since we, her kids, have left home, Mom handwrites us a letter sometimes twice a week, depending on the volume of news, a letter being borne out of the sensation that life is too voluminous to be embodied by anything more than flyaway stretches of news. She writes them longhand on loose leaf, then drives to town to make photocopies at ten cents per page at the library, then mails them off in envelopes covered in stickers: an oval sticker with lilies and *Behold the beauty of the Lord*, or a sticker of a squirrel pinning each of the letters in *HELLO THERE* on a laundry line.

Her letters do feel like embodiment—hers and ours. Her letters bear her body, an incarnation of her and her voice and the things her hands have touched today; and her letters bear our bodies, or at least our faces as they're conjured in her mind as she writes. She writes the mundane and the revelation; she writes whether it's beef roast or beans, whether it's the cripple's faith or the apostle's that really brought healing in the Book of Acts; she reports on C.S.'s health and sketches the layout for this spring's garden (where the sweet corn and pumpkins will go, the tomatoes and pole beans, and the perimeter of marigolds and zinnias). She writes of how the yellow colt's feet are popping up along the ditch and how the world is glowing there and she wishes we were there to see it, too. She wishes we were there.

October 31, she writes in an update, *did ten loads of clothes (electric had been off a week), hung eight out. November 2: Finished the ironing—a coon tried to get in the chicken house—tore one chicken's leg off before your dad could get out there to shoot it—weighed every bit twenty pounds! Have separated the chicken out—using Vicks, Porters, and Bag Balm— name: Henrietta Mae.*

In the next line: *I'm taking a lot of comfort in Acts 17:26-28. I'm thinking everyone is where they are for good reason and the main one being so that you all would seek God's face even more. The truth is: He truly is not far from each one of us and it really is that 'in Him we live and move and have our being.'*

Sometimes she gets preachy, or plagued with self-doubt, or, most often, both at once. Sometimes she falls asleep as she writes and leaves a smudge of ink, a word half-dream.

In her weaker moments, she begs us to move back home, clinging to the image of each of our houses sprouting up from the ground all around her like barley. But when she's stronger, the letters themselves seem to suffice. The letters say with confidence: *your day, however spent, is now joined to mine, and it has been a good day.*

On the loose leaf from Dollar General, her letters often begin with *Well*— as though we'd spoken only a moment ago, as though she's starting the day alongside us and the present tense of the letter is fused with the present of the reading.

Dear All, she begins on November 20, Saturday, *Well, I had this revelation from the Lord and even though I kind of choked on it, I feel like I have to let you fellas know about it.*

Another begins: *Well, yesterday was a very sad day.*

Another: *Well, we have around six inches of snow.*

Well, it seems like I can't get all my thoughts together and at the same time make the trek to town.

Well, Ashley is 17 years old today!

These letters are her closest thing to a diary. But, for her, a letter is not a record; it is speaking. A voice without recorder. She tells us not to keep them; they'll clutter; just put them in the recycling, she says, or use the backs of them for scrap paper, and sometimes I do. But usually I keep her letters. (I have them spread out, now, on my desk.) I keep them in order, I archive; I keep notes on how she makes her meaning, notes which I'll be ever comparing with my own. She lives the length of the day while I often feel that I flit, a moth in the world; Mom emanates light, a wick soaked long in kerosene. I cannot help but keep her letters in a folder that documents her winter, details how she cares for C.S., my granddad, her letter, in its saying, a tiny history of her grief and her joy—entrusted to me.

To her, the letters are simply a way to draw our faces into her circle of light.

In truth, her photocopied print-cursive hybrid can halt my hands from writing manuscripts. Implicit in her letter is the wonderful, dreadful news: I could burn this letter today—and this essay—and be ash with its ash.

When C.S. dies and the sympathy cards come in, she loves each of them and tears off their lovely sentimental covers, writes on their undersides and sends them as postcards.

Her letters do not simply blur her present with my present; they blur time with time, the temporal with the eternal. *Beloved,* she reminds me from a New Testament epistle, *do not forget this one thing, that with the Lord one day is as a thousand years, and a thousand years as one day.*

Mom is aging. I notice it the way you notice the sky getting darker earlier in September. I want to be able to let her age, which means I want to let myself age. She's sixty-two, and I thirty-one. She does not long for her younger self; she is okay with aging, since she believes in an eternity that already grows green and firm like pith inside her aging body. When the time comes to go, she'll simply slip into a new body, still carrying on the same conversation. She'll keep going for fifty-minute walks, her litanies strewn all the way down Wilson Hill and back.

Well, she begins on October 26, *one more page and hopefully I'll send this out tomorrow.*

My laundry is soaked through now, bending the clothesline toward the ground with weight, with gravity and rain.

She's dying, my mother, but so am I. Not soon, but soon. This day will bear fruit, and that fruit will be the death of us, a good death. What makes a day good? Perhaps a good day is a good full death. I hear her insist: *You will not die alone.* Is that possible—to not be alone in death? Is that what makes a death good? That it be attended? Is what makes for a good death the accumulation of good days? But, again, what makes for a good day? It is sometimes for me: I wrote something true. A good day somehow looms larger than Time, yet a day is so small, perhaps too small a unit to measure and too meager a handful of coinage to squander.

I think of Socrates in his last hours, all the women shooed from his room, for they would surely make a fuss while he practiced his earnest dying, drinking his hemlock to die the best death. And often we say it is a good death if bloodless, hardly noticed, dying in your sleep with no faces hovering, no last rites or final words, no disturbance. But, for my mother—one day she is swimming all afternoon in the Atlantic; too self-conscious for a bathing suit, she learns from my sister how to get changed from her blouse into a tank top, on a public beach, wondering, amazed, in what context her daughter has learned this skill of changing in public—and it's nothing but her and the water's surface and then, deep beneath, long colorless tusks of life growing upward toward light—miles through water, her flippering legs. She loves, loves to disturb the waters, to slice through with her body, all the while her hospice-heart, her hospice-lips moving with the words of the sick and the dying—*catheter, IV, Lasix, colostomy, dressing* and *undressing* and *dressing the wounds.* In her house, death will not be shut away quietly in a closet. There she is, propelling herself between the great shafts of light, among the reefs, troubling the ocean waters. Death is with us, rending us, binding us, and she is with the dying, midway on the path, a steward of their deaths, a midwife even—if that is possible. To midwife the dead. For C.S., she wipes the celery-seed dressing from his cracked lips; she hears his confessions. And even now her own father's lungs fill with blood, her own mother falls backward from the flowerbed to shatter her wrist, the diabetic neighbor loses toes and limbs pinched off by kidneys failing on dialysis—Mom's face is there, the moon rising above the other's face that is the moon's reflection.

Night

It's true she makes the day last long, likes to lengthen and slow it and put off the night, but love of life and fear of death—they are not the same thing.

The Bible is all she reads—*with the Lord one day is as a thousand years, and a thousand years as one day*—but I know of a few exceptions that she brings out at night, such as a few Christian romances; such as the novel she is sometimes writing, hidden in a garbage bag in the closet, the narrative taking place over one single week, the days elongated as though the project itself might slow time with its particulars; such as Harriet Arnow's novel from the Fifties, *The Dollmaker* (though she is not interested in Jane Fonda's feminist film adaptation). Mom doesn't own Arnow's book, just keeps checking it out of the library in town, and their only copy is a large-print edition.

That last chapter, she reads in bed: Clovis, having moved his family from Kentucky to Detroit for factory work, is on strike, the children know better than to ask for more milk, and Gertie gets an order for fifty-dollars' worth of wooden dolls for a church Christmas bazaar. She needs good wood and has a block of the best cherry that she's been carving in their dank apartment, letting the shavings snow down to the floor late into the night. Out of the block she's carved a man with an empty uplifted hand, a head but no face. She takes her boy Amos, pulls her statue in the boy's wagon to the wood lot, asks the scrap-wood man to saw the statue into boards for the dolls she's to whittle. The head of the statue must be split apart with an ax first, and the man can't do it, knowing the soul she's put into her carving, so she does it herself—and either she or the wood lets out a yelp as the ax splits the blank face right off the head of the carved figure. The scrap-wood man rubs his hand over the blank faceand says to Gertie that she meant it to be Christ, didn't she? But she could find no face? Gertie shakes her head, no, so many faces would have done fine, millions fine enough for him, the faces of neighbors in the alley, any would have done.

The large-print edition makes a tent over Mom as she reads in bed till her forearms ache, or till the book slips down to rest on her head and

Dad gently takes it from her hands.

They sleep beside C.S.'s hospital bed in the living room, on the sofa bed. Mom often wakes while C.S. and Dad sleep, as she did when we kids all slept in the house and she rose to tend the beans in the pressure canner that rattled with jittery gunshots. Then, the coming of daybreak never occurred for her alone. Watching the day come was like letting a face come clear, closer and closer, always a face with a signature square jaw or hazel eyes or dry lips moving with breath.

It's a beautiful October when C.S. dies. Mom wants to sleep on the sofa bed one more night, by his empty hospital bed. Dad doesn't understand, but says okay and holds her. "It's just for tonight," she says. "Let the oxygen machine run, just for tonight."

Writing into the night, I've drunk half a Killian's Red, and so much has happened—time is so vast—much good and much bad. (I know she does not like me drinking.) My friend Kevin has emailed that he's found the poverty harsher in his travels in Cambodia than he has anywhere—Pakistan, Burma. Young women in dirty camisoles proposition him and seem to sprout on the arms of men all over the city. This happened during my swallow: a woman has wrung her hands while a man whom she does not know and who does not ask her name unbuckles his belt. And my mother has wiped celery-seed dressing from C.S.'s chin after supper and has heard the confessional flutters of his dreams. Someone has lit a lamp; someone has burned like a wick; I have put the bottle to my lips and heard a skunk and her babies rustle outside in the trash bins, and have kept writing.

We're different, Mom and I. But not so different. The difference lies in the work we've chosen. She stows food in canning jars, bathes the ailing. I stow words in files and those files on a hard drive, and I go untouched by hands for many hours at a time.

But my laundry hangs black-wet on the line tonight, and I'm still a girl with my sister on a summer night when the day has been long, the length of the burn of the small brushfire by the barn. The loose walnut leaves, which have batted smoke toward the wet cotton of the sheets, have stilled. And, as though reading their stillness like a sign, my mother says she is too tired to take in the sheets from the line, so we leave them to hang overnight. We sleep on our cool bare mattresses then, mine next to my sister's, covered over top with some sheets from the closet, untucked. It is the gift of something temporary, a night without a made-up bed, a result of not having strength to finish a task. I wrap the closet-sheet around me, because, if I don't, I might slip off the bed, into the unknown. We've burnt some brush and trash, and we've shelled some of the walnuts, and we've half-done the laundry—what work has made of us today is finally allowed to be laid down, cooled and (as we imagined) beautiful. We smell only the old sheets that cover us—blue once, and, I remember now, dotted with tiny flowers—they smell of musty waiting. While our other sheets sleep pinned up outside and break the stillness only once or twice to flap, as if to tell us something through the window screen. Downstairs, Mom finishes with her bath, the powdery scent of her Jean Naté coming close, the porch light switched off. I pull back a corner of the closet-sheet and sleep with the cool mattress touching my cheek.

They are ghosts, the bed sheets on the line, hailing our deaths, our brevity. We lie down to rest, we are the same. I sometimes fear that I'll make no mark or I'll miss the vital thing, or my apartment will be sucked up into a Midwest tornado and all my work and me with it. The thought of dying, not soon, but soon. Mom lives with no thought to permanence, but not because she thinks she'll live forever—there's no denying the lungs full of fluid and the neighbor's toes then limbs lost one by one. I know (and she knows) that she will cling as everyone clings, with a startled look or a *But*— on her lips, when she dies. Even so: to be, to love, to work, to set down a bucket and run. *Well*— and so on goes her conversation with the world.

And in the midst of her thick humid days, she is hot and malleable as iron in the fire—ever changing, running out of the bathroom with her hair half-combed, half-dried upside-down by the wall-heater, squinting without her glasses—*Two things*, she writes on her loose leaf, her face glowing from either the revelation or the heat from the heater. *Number one: don't let anything rob you of your joy, and, number two, I'm really sorry for pestering you kids to come home. I will try to do better.*

And in the midst of her brittle autumn days, she breathes, exhales the name of God, *YHWH*, with voiceless breath—that name derived from the Hebrew verb to be. *YHWH* is her I AM, the One who is, the eternal present. *YHWH* is the clutching of the dog gone slack in hands made old and rough by wash water. *YHWH* made strange with the familiar strangeness of a porch light, Tingley boots, and a nightgown draped with a black sweater. She slips inside the name of God, hushed by the pulse. And inside the name of God, it's as if we live a thousand years in a day—the day itself an ancient thing. Perhaps we do it without knowing it, the way the weaver of a thousand rugs knows only the reds and blues of this rug she weaves, though her hands ache with the thousands. And the way, for Mom, there is the face right before her, etched with pain or with bruised sleep. There is no other.

It's getting so late and I could burn this. And I might do it, too, or I might send it to Mom who will read it standing by the stove with her lipstick-rouged face and tank top dirty with garden soil and, over top of it, my fifth-grade jean jacket she can still wear, sleeves rolled up, and she will call me and say that my work is good, except there's too much of her in it. Except that she didn't know someone was watching her.

Very late at night, her rough hands are made smooth as she lotions

C.S.'s arms, Lubriderm always, making both their ancient skins, finally, child-supple. She has smeared Porters Ointment on the sore of the isolated one-legged chicken, has put its food and water out in cottage cheese containers. She listens, unable to sleep as the moon rises then fades, to a sermon tape from the Bible Believer's Commentary. It's a tiny-voiced woman named Edith tracing the Lamb of God throughout the Scriptures. Mom is sleepless over the way the Lamb will come back, with the new worlds, the new heaven and the new earth—what the form, what the voice, what the day—the day of the Lord. And she's ardent that the day of the Lord is *this* day, for they blur. What face but this face?

I have stayed up all night writing. And now it is dawn, again.

So Great a Cloud | *Josephine*

The imperfect is our paradise.
Note that, in this bitterness, delight,
since the imperfect is so hot in us,
lies in flawed words and stubborn sounds.

—Wallace Stevens, "Poems of Our Climate"

1

A woman wearing a ratty black slip has entered my prayers. Thick
eyeliner, pack of Pall Malls, combat boots. She got in through a crack
in the wall and now she's looking out through the window slats—for
what? She lies back on the bed and buoys her breasts with her forearm,
smoking hands-free, lazy. I was saying something before—please or
sorry, or maybe mouthing the word mercy—but the prayer is all silence
now. I watch her. She doesn't behave like she's uninvited. She wears no
socks with her too-big boots, as if she only slipped them on to step out
into the snow for a minute, to get the mail. I think about kicking her out,
but we just stare and stare. She wins, and I'm stuck; my thoughts trail off
then sharpen, as if she's nudging them in a certain direction. (Lazy, but
pushy.) I think in fragments—about the story of the girl who gave rice
milk to Siddhartha so he could stay put under the tree and Become, how
he took her rice milk for a sign, how she took care that it didn't sour, kept
it cool in the shade—did she lick her lips, thirsty? I think of the Prophet
Isaiah: come buy wine and milk without money. Could be the girl licked
her lips but still held out the thin bark bowl to him who drank it down.
They that thirst, they that buy the milk, they that give it—whose is the
holiness? Is that the question Black Nylon is here to pose? Is that my

question? Not quite, but it's close. I'm not even neighbor to the camp of the Enlightened, I'm just saying there are many who tend us and don't they lean in close and don't they breathe on our skin to remind us of something?

Black Nylon reminds me of something. With such clarity do the eyes lined in black look at me.

I don't know how to end my prayer.

I'm just saying hello.

2

I sit down to pray then sit down to write. Two tasks sometimes without much boundary. The cheeky invader of my morning prayers stays with me at my desk, blows smoke in my face. She is a pesky vision. Her smoke clouds around me and I think the phrase: *cloud of witnesses.* Well, okay. What about it?

From the Bible's Epistle to the Hebrews: "Therefore we also, since we are surrounded by so great a cloud of witnesses." It's a Scripture I've known since childhood, like a scrap of fabric among other scraps that I'd quilt with if I knew how to quilt, that I keep in a soft sack of odds and ends, wrap a pebble in for a gift and tie the top.

Here's my scrap: cloud of witnesses, the phrase cycling through my mind. And though I am frittering away my work time, I go ahead and wonder: what witnesses? Back to the Epistle to the Hebrews: "They were stoned and tormented, sawn in two, wandered in deserts and mountains, obtained a good testimony through faith, but didn't receive a promise, God having provided something better for us, that they should not be made perfect apart from us." So the witnesses were the bony martyrs at the dawn of the Church—metal-colored faces, worn, shriveled for the desert birds to pick their meat, flesh not able to shimmer back into word because we don't go backwards. (The Word became Flesh and there's no going back.)

It's time I get to the short story draft. But now I wonder: why are these witnesses not made perfect without us? And what is the nature of that perfection? And who are all the other witnesses? Who's my cloud? *Who's my cloud?* I know my current project must wait.

3

It's a writer's question, but to sit with it I must also sit with the Scripture (the scrap of Hebrews) that provokes me—not to study it but to sense it. For the Word became Flesh and there's no going back—it yielded itself to biopsy, ran fever, fell faint. What I mean is:

There's what the Bible says then there's the flesh that the word becomes, indisputable, with a pulse and blood. I can't account for it; I can't exegete that heartbeat and song's refrain—the Scriptures that cycle through—the way my fingers remember, in time, the thumb roll on the banjo, sounds souring—the way the Scriptures are true like your pee-puddle is true on the playground, hot, calling for a fresh pair of pants. Indisputable flesh, the thigh that bears the gush. No going back. Word is flesh and must be sensed: it tastes hears sees touches blesses and dresses. Catches the scent. *Yields itself to biopsy.* Trying to sense this Scripture like a mole its next tunnel turn, I think: and whose hands do you reach for, Flesh, when at the mercy of The Biopsy Report? When it comes back abnormal? Maybe you reach for your cloud of witnesses—you reach for that one to bring you into the circle. She calls you "Baby."

4

Josephine. I believe she's the first member of my cloud of witnesses.

"Baby" she called me. What else do I know of Josephine? I know it was her idea to have a taffy pull. Something exotic, saltwater taffy like the kind she had brought back to West Virginia from Ocean City, in bite sizes twisted into Easter papers: taffy held in the mouth for a long time, under the tongue, before chewing. Something for us kids in the Whetsell Settlement to do instead of prowling the Ames parking lot in pickups. Stir the taffy to toughness then pull it taut until tiny white gems would snap loose; someone would bring the tissue paper to wrap it, ribbons to tie the tops.

But I don't think the taffy pull ever happened, for one reason or another. I don't really know if that taffy Josephine gave me came all the way from the Ocean City Boardwalk, some bright beach shop, or from a gumball machine. But I know she was dreaming things up for me, and for all the kids in our tiny rural community. Josie was dreaming us up a safe and beautiful place that could live and shimmer inside our regular place, and it did feel safe. And those other women on the screened-in porch were dreaming too, making plans for this taffy pull under a fog of cigarette smoke too thick to leak out the screens, hoarse-talking about the kettle and the confectioner's sugar and the way the Settlement boys were headed for Hades and another DUI. Josephine in a tight leopard bodysuit and jeans and ice-pink lipstick and "Baby" she called me— wasn't I so little, too little to know what these women would mean to me?—"Baby, you can tie the ribbons on the tops," she said, "once the taffy cools."

5

Why her? Why is Josie in my cloud—and she is witness to what?

My memories of Jo are inaccurate and sharp at once. Sheets of siding that don't match, that porch walled with screen, and a rutted road, hens in the ruts. I saw her in groups of women, a cloud, a cluster. Dramatic wave of her hand and a calling out in her smoker's voice—not a call-and-response shout, because it needed no answer; it was final, Josephine's call, it was brawny. Her earrings dangled strands dipped in dirty moonlight; sometimes she came to Beatty Church, sometimes she got mad and walked out. "Baby" she'd call me, Kool-Aid she'd pour me at Bible School, when she and church were on good terms, and engulf me in cigarette smoke and spandex leopard skin arms. Josephine. What a space she made for me when I was boyish and bone, all wire and worry and wonder—"Baby, come on up here"—hissing teeth at her sons rolling off to the Ames parking lot. "Them boys is my death"— I knew she loved them terribly.

I'm there sipping my Kool-Aid with my Bible School craft she taught me—popsicle-stick cross. The glue is weak; my cross is coming apart. "Miss Josephine," I say, holding up the sticks with gold glitter dusting down from them—she lights up, looks at the new moon, hums a dirty song. "It's okay, Baby."

Josie is a member of the female cluster-cloud of my mountain childhood. When I got married—surprising myself and them—they sewed me a hen-print clothespin holder, embroidered me a pillow, held a wedding shower as an initiation ceremony I neither wanted nor expected. These were women who wouldn't go to church if they had no nylons to wear, or if, in Jo's case, somebody one pew over had been uppity. Sentimental sayings, crisp judgment, sure, clannish, sure, but wide wide arms.

That's why. Why she's in my cloud of witnesses—wide open leopard skin arms offering me their strength and mercy—and witness to the world as I live in it. She's witness to the world as I try to write it, manifest it. Its details, but more than the details too— witness to some perfection within that world, within us. These women are not made perfect apart from me, nor I apart from them.

6

Miss Josephine: I suspect that the composition of my witness-cloud determines the tenor and timbre of my work. That cloud's population density, its demographic, whose names are on the membership roll.

Whom, in the dark at my desk, do I write for? That's the core of my question.

And, even more to the point, when revealed and tested by the witnesses' fire, will my art stand?

I am always in company when I write. I write for the deepest part of me, yes, but down deep, there's a host, a ragtag crew. Most of these people are not there by invitation, I can't help that. But, by my own volition, I can choose whom to invite close-up, an inner circle to surround me in the mist, neighbors strung tight by tin-can phones. These are folks to whom I can make myself accountable to say things true. Tell the story true. I think I'm writing for them. And by true I mean, not factual, but honest, in keeping with the world as I live in it and not some nostalgic or cheap or aestheticized version of it. True as in received out from what that world is willing to give and not imposed upon it. (True as in Miss Josephine could find herself at home in the story, unabstracted, unobscured, in full flesh.)

There are others in my host whose voices only dwarf and hollow me and convince me to write what's false. Some are abstractions: the Publisher, the Market, the Conference, the Academy. Not really specific people, but the idea of them—the Judge and Executioner, the Critic and Reviewer. Okay, some in particular too: the rich uncle I always wanted to prove my metal against, the professor who wrote his corrections onto my thoughts even as I thought them, the pretty girl who believed me shabby in my best sweater. And also some clamoring voices of my own: the self in me that seeks a perfection that is enemy to the good, isolating and merciless; the self that says I'm a genius deserving my place in the sun, and the one that says I'm worm dung. In my host, these folks are only there for me to impress and prove wrong, to compete with and perform for and prove saleable to. They make demands on me I cannot fulfill and they turn my art to *tinfoil* and *trash*. And by tinfoil and trash I mean work that wraps itself around a successful trend and takes on that outer shape, the way foil does, without taking on the substance. I mean stories whose shapes I polish anxiously without attending to their secret interiors. I mean stories that are derivative and forced (stories in which Josie might find herself caricature, her voice all emptied of brawn, her body only an idea of itself).

But my cloud, my cloud of witnesses in the inner circle drawn close, they demand of me what I need most to offer. My best offerings and also the yoking of my offerings with those of the ready world. My cloud waits for words that take on flesh, not shadows, off-key and skittish.

Don't waste time on work that is not your work, they say. You're a mother bear; your cloud's your cubs, your cubs your cloud. I must say to all the others in my vaster host: "Don't you mess with my cloud. I won't kick you out, for I do not wish to be inhospitable and, besides, there's no getting rid of you. You may come in and sit quietly in the corner, but you can't put the hot breath to my skin, no. It's Josie's got that place, that right, our beautiful taffy still hot in the kettle, saltwater burning our eyes."

It's she who will help me say something that needs saying and will demand that I say it with my truest timbre and tone. (Could be that, once Josie and my cloud make me stronger, I'll spend some time with those nasty folks on the outer edges of my inner host, like the pretty girl who snubbed me and my sweater, and perhaps even they are not made perfect without me, nor I without them—but that's for when I'm further along.)

To say that your cloud's membership determines your work's quality is to admit that the integrity of your art is bound up with those you choose to draw nearest to you, and to acknowledge that there are some that shore up your lie, some your truth. That is, some that dress you up in laughable ill-fitting suits and some that want you to breathe and flow in the housedress that fits you perfectly. This is a hard idea to put into words; I guess that's why it keeps slipping back toward body.

7

So who else? There are the constant witnesses, like Josephine and the women on the porches of my childhood—Cindy, Eliza, Liz, Jessie B., Aimee—and there are those that come into my cloud for only a short time. Like the women I gathered with in a Philadelphia kitchen, for Spanish rice and *café con leche* and heartbreak. Like a few of my students. The girl with high hair and a story and a poem or two that she wrote through the night. The young guy fighting acne and drawing the map of his universe for me, on my desk—his warlocks and larwocks and their intergalactic battles—utterly lost between his stars. A few are so beautifully inky-wet, all I can say is, "Will you come be in my cloud? Leave your muddy clogs at the door, the fire and soup are hot. Let's help each other do our best work as it brims from us." And they do; they keep my work young and vulnerable.

Who else?

When I visited a jail for the first time—those guys in orange jumpsuits—some came into my cloud. Like the one leading us in the breathing exercise: "Put your right hand over your heart, your left hand on your stomach—breathe in—breathe out—breathe in—breathe out—

repeat after me: *I am here*—again, softer: *I am here*—again, softer: *I am here.*" He had hurt someone badly and was very sorry, eyes fixed on the sealed envelope of mercy. Cloud of witnesses: bear witness, remind me of mercy, that I might not simply mouth the word but sound it out with full-bodied sound.

And there are shelves of books in my cloud, too, writers whose pen strokes I am following, their narrow channel. I draw them near me, for it's not only whom you write for—giving your offering—it's also those you write *because of*, because of the path that's been carved by their rivers of ink and the way they enable you to branch out into your own trickle then stream.

8

And that woman in the ratty black slip. I cannot forget her. She started this whole thing.

"Hello," she says back to me, back in my room of prayer, watching me skeptically but with absolute and severe love, that clarity. Combat boots indisputable. Looks out through my window slats again—yes, I see what she's looking for now—she sees the altar-called girl, the little scared one inside me, pee-hot, hell-fired and feeling more pressure than a pressure cooker full of jars of beans, pressure for perfection and spotlessness. I see that this sorry young thing is the one who often courts the voices that ought not to be in my cloud—"O Judge, O Executioner," she grovels. "O Critic of Critics."

Black Nylon won't stand for it.

She opens the window, says, "Come here, Hon, come on up here." Wide-open arms like Josephine's, easy and easing that poor girl. "You got to let go." Rice milk maid, floozy saint. A significant, if imaginary, member of my cloud. She does not coddle; she keeps me clear and dry and steady.

9

And there are my sisters. And the man who accompanied our church choir on banjo without reading a single sheet of tablature. And my friend who cried when he saw the birdseed set out for abandoned baby pigeons in Paris. And the man I married on a Settlement garden plot grown over with August crabgrass, holding a gladiola and refusing to regret this, no matter what would happen. And my rival in church choir. And Aunt Kathy always dialing our house. And Gaye, stiff, brittle and cool with judgment, self-righteous—but she left fifty dollars in our mailbox once when we kids were sick and had no medicine.

And there are more, but I'll stop there.

Somehow they each help me write the truer story.

Most in my cloud don't even know they're in my cloud. Probably never will. Most come from where I come from, the hollows and ridges, some from where I've been since—DC and Philadelphia, the Midwest, the Northwest—some from my book stacks, some from where I live now. Some are dreamed up, in whole or in part. Many are dead. Every one of them makes me homesick for the home inside myself—a spacious place with biscuits aplenty and with cool, cool milk I could never buy. A few might well beg off, wishing to be elsewhere and not stuck with me. Still, I call on them. They are not made perfect without me.

10

What, finally, *is* this perfection that's mentioned in the Scripture-scrap of Hebrews and that's part of my sensing-out of the Scripture's pulse and throb? When I call upon the cloud, "Please don't dissipate. Please help me tell it straight, or if crooked, help smooth the bends in the road like pulling out the taffy soft and warm"—when I stand with this cloud whose promise of the perfect is bound up with mine, whose word is flesh and flesh grass, the perfection we're promised may be, simply, the fact of our binding. Face unto face, hot breath. Terrifically flawed, we work hard side by side to make the things made, our gifts gifted, and we are enough.

The Helicopter | *My Cousin*

During the hottest dog days of August, Betty mixed biscuits wearing only a bra and slip, no matter who was around. Outside the screen door of the house in Spencer, the kids squatted to shoot marbles—a yarn-string circle in the driveway dust, one kid thumbing the aggie and launching it toward the prettiest cat's eye with the orange and black ribboned center. When the aim was good, the aggie smacked the cat's eye and sent it flying to the dog's dent in the dirt under the porch. It rolled to the center like a bead in a dish, and the dog went after it for his own. The kids' grandma stood by and watched, too old to sweat in her blue polyester housedress with three-quarter sleeves. She clutched her left arm with her right and looked uncomfortable in town; she watched the street the way a kid watches the closet for a specter. She went for the screen door when she heard banging pans and cussing, to help Betty with supper.

These are my mother's people, the Boggs family, on her mother's side. Down in Spencer, West Virginia, in Roane County, which is a four-hour drive south from my childhood home in the northern part of the state, people say the mountains get meaner. They get fiercer the farther south you go, closing you up into their wet heat and shrinking the sky so you can't breathe when you look up. It's dark too early, even in summer. Mom's parents had moved north so that Granddad could take a job with the power company in Albright, West Virginia. But, as a kid, Mom loved to go south, to let herself be swallowed by the more severe mountains each time her parents were willing to take her. As a mother, she told me the stories about her uncle Harry and aunt Betty, Betty's scant clothes in the heat, cousins who taught Mom to shoot marbles in a squat.

After my grandparents moved north to a house just outside of town on Albright Road, my granddad's choice piece of advice to his kids was to "get the hell out." Out of West Virginia altogether, he meant. A harsh imperative, but who would fault him—the youngest of thirteen, a brother or two in the state penitentiary, a suffocating matriarch who tried to guilt all her kids into staying under her roof. Jobs are too scarce, he said, and the people too backward. But Mom's small sprig of a body put down surprisingly deep roots. Even in her teens, when her parents announced they were leaving their house on Albright Road for a brick house with hedges in town, Mom strapped herself to the support beam in the basement and refused to leave till they forced her. And she was reluctant to go off to college, to move up in the world the way they wanted her to, but eventually she obliged.

Mom's deepest roots reached to Spencer. Whenever she went down to visit, she stayed with her grandma Boggs on the farm. She shadowed her grandma, followed her blue housedress around as though it were the surest thing in sight. Some of my mom's people, like Aunt Betty, stayed in the small town, and she would visit with them and with Aunt Susie's bunch, who had moved to the neighboring town of the peculiar name Looneyville. But most of the family left, moved to Ohio or took jobs in Kentucky near the university, returning home only for an occasional wedding, a funeral, and the Boggs Reunion in late summer.

For us kids, Mom's stories from Spencer had a rosy hue; she left out the unkindnesses, the particular breed of spite or shame that brewed in her relations and took them north. She left out the story someone later whispered to me, about her cousin who went after his own sister with scissors. It's not that Mom was ignorant of the more sinister details of her family; she just took those details for granted. They were not to get in the way. Love covered over a multitude of belittling remarks and unsettling secrets. My mother was bound to her people.

My great-uncle and great-aunt, Harry and Betty, hosted the Boggs Reunion most years. They married young, inherited the Boggs farm and hated it. So they moved to town and Harry got work drilling gas wells and made pretty good money. Before Grandma and Granddaddy Boggs died, they sent him to pilot school for a time, and it was enough to put the love of flight in him. He bought a helicopter to keep in a hangar at Roane County's tiny airport. It may have been his own way of getting the hell out. He and Betty lived maxed out in debt in Spencer, raised their kids and sent them out to make something of themselves.

The first Boggs Reunion that I remember was in August of 1984 when I was five. Betty called Mom and asked her to be in charge of games for the kids. Thrilled, Mom drove to Family Dollar and bought a big mesh sack of glass marbles, cat's eyes with the ribbons suspended in their centers. She cut up scraps of muslin and sewed forty or so tiny drawstring bags. I helped her puff-paint Boggs Reunion, 1984 on each bag and then filled each with marbles. I got mine early and emptied the little sack into my jeans pocket for the car ride down to Spencer.

That year, Harry and Betty had rented the 4-H summer camp in Roane County for the reunion. When we pulled up to the dining hall, people were streaming in and out of the screened-in porch, hugging and talking, hands on hips or on Tupperware containers of food. Kid cousins congregated on the steps and then raced off in clumps toward something beyond the hall. I didn't know many of my second cousins, so I was a while understanding that everyone there was my kin. But I recognized Aunt Unabelle on the steps at once, and she came over and plucked me from the car, up into her arms and into her smell of old blouse and old skin.

"Wait till you see it!" one of the boy cousins hollered to another, running around the dining hall's corner. Mom hauled out her box of marble bags from the trunk and asked Unabelle what the ruckus was about. Oh, Harry's landed his helicopter, Unabelle told us, he parked it over on the baseball field past the cabins, promised to give the kids rides after supper.

At the news, my sister and brothers darted after the other kids. I squirmed loose from Unabelle's arms in time to turn the corner with them. Too short, I had to fight through the herd of kids to finally get a good look. And there it was in the field. I stopped cold and broke into a quick sweat. I went no closer to it right then. The helicopter gleamed like something from another world, sitting out past second base. It was a deep glossy yellow on its sides, the kind of yellow you might lick for honey, but it was mostly glass in front, even halfway along the bottom where your feet would go. The chopper blades spun in a lazy twirl, as though Uncle Harry had just started it up to get a rise out of the kids and then shut it back off again to make them wait, to make us wait and sweat. He was walking toward the dining hall now, flanked by giddy boys getting first dibs on rides, and I heard him say that we'd have to wait till after supper. He said we'd be able to look through the glass floor and see Spencer shrink back like God's little model; we'd see as God sees, the pastures like quilt patches, the people like ants.

I still hadn't moved. Harry walked past me and winked, patted my girl head, like a puppy's, and the cousins swarmed by. Someone was calling us for supper. I breathed in the heavy humid Spencer air, so close to my cousins that I couldn't tell the scent of my sweat from theirs.

Before following the swarm back to the dining hall, I noticed one older cousin who stood apart from the rest. He was a huge boy I didn't know, with a face a little on a slant, black hair cut coarse. His arms bounced a bit at his sides, like he might have been flapping new wings. He looked at me, and I scrambled after the other kids into the screen-porch of the dining hall.

***

Today, in this Midwest town where I live, I read a chunk from a ratty paperback copy of *The Cloud of Unknowing*, written by an anonymous fourteenth-century mystic. A sentence sticks to me like a burr: *Strike with the sharp dart of longing love—and do not leave it no matter what happens.* I'm surprised by it, since I haven't been on board for much of the text and haven't felt anything from the book strike a chord within me. I have been thinking about changing the way I live, a thought that always moves me to read bright-eyed mystics, poets, Buddhists and Sufis and Quakers, to try for a new angle. So I dog-ear the page and take the book with me as I head out the door to take my car in for an oil change.

In the lobby at the Jiffy Lube, after handing over my car key, I sit down and puzzle over what I've read, as though fiddling with the burr. Where is it that I'm supposed to strike with the sharp dart exactly? In the book, the anonymous writer seems to mean strike the very Cloud of Unknowing itself, the cloud between self and God. From what I can tell, the cloud the writer describes is a sort of dread that takes your ego down a few notches. Or obliterates it altogether. You stand in it naked, with nothing to recommend you. Go deep into the dread, the writer urges. Face your own weakness and nothingness, your own fraught story; stay constant and look neither to the right nor to the left for escape. Sit with it and do not rise, and do not unfix your sharp dart of a gaze from what longing love reveals. No matter what.

I wait in the Jiffy Lube lobby with two other customers. "Judge Alex" comes onto the TV that's bolted to the wall, and the three of us get sucked in. It's a petty claims court show, and it seems that, during a commercial break, a commotion started brewing in the courtroom. Judge Alex pounds his gavel, grinning. His black hair is slicked back and looks good. He's presiding over a crude, stagey sort of case: a disheveled woman with dark roots but a white-orange ponytail complains at high pitch about her husband's affair with her neighbor—and who has the right to keep the apartment, the mini-dish, the DVDs? And she's tired of cooking his meals when he's banging the blonde next door. The deadbeat husband surprises us—me and the two guys in the lobby—when he doesn't deny the affair at all, but confirms it and claims that his wife is verbally abusive; she drove him to it, he says, and he has every right to stay in the apartment, and even to seek therapy at her expense.

She's weaving back and forth now like an Apostolic churchgoer who's got the Spirit. She looks like she might leap over the railing to smack him, but instead she glowers, ignoring the slick Judge Alex altogether when he tries to interject, though he seems happy enough for what the fight could do for his ratings.

She says, "Then you keep the place and give me a damn settlement and I'll get the hell out—and we'll see how you do—I'm getting the hell out." She hugs herself and looks about to bawl. I find myself in her corner, cheering her on like all the folks in the courtroom are doing, their hooting bringing down the judge's gavel again. I can almost see her taking flight, shedding this drag of a husband and rising above it all, letting her hair go natural, making something of herself the way she's supposed to. But she does in fact start to cry. Though I suspect these shows are scripted, I can't help but think she means it, that she's really getting out, and she looks out of place with her sincerity. She wears a flannel shirt buttoned up halfway, looks like an oversized child who doesn't want to leave just yet, but is too stubborn to let it show. It shows, despite her. And the camera zooms in close on the lines in her face, the lines that suggest it's not about the husband, not really. It's the stale air of the cheap apartment, it's the sagging flesh of her face. It's the threadbare Budweiser T-shirt she wears underneath the flannel; she wears it for the comfort of the familiar, though the familiar is what's killing her. The mechanic behind the desk calls my name before I can sort out my thoughts about the woman. He calls my name a second time. I sign the receipt for the oil change, get in my car and go, without hearing the judge's ruling.

The woman's icy words grate against me in the car—*I'm getting the hell out.* I suppose she and I aren't in the same boat at all, but maybe we're in the same choppy waters. She reminds me of my granddad telling us all to leave home, to succeed and rise. When he said it, you could see the wear of forty years of watching pressure gauges at the Albright Power Plant start to show in his square face. And I suppose I did what he said, to some extent; at this moment I do live away from the mountains. But I don't always feel an easiness about it. Where are you supposed to go when you *get out*? When you make your way? In this small city of people where I live now, the house windows that I drive by glow clear in early evening. Before people drop their Venetian blinds, they're so vulnerable; you can see into them and make your own guesses about what it is they want out of, to fly from, what they are making of themselves or not making of themselves. What they might do when they face their own dread, whether they'll stay with it—their longing taking on shape and dimension—no matter what happens.

I pull into my apartment lot and know that there is a part of me that goes after flight. I remember slipping a quarter into a gumball machine at the Ames Department Store as a kid and getting back a bubble-case. Inside the case: a tiny aluminum Pegasus charm, bent a little on one wing. I fell in love with it, but never put it on a chain around my neck. I buried it, thinking that was the necessary step to take to set it free for flight, to make it become a real heaving horse with a ten-foot wingspan. My heart sank when I dug it up the next week, still a dinky charm with a damaged wing. Another time, I believed my sister when she told me the sand dollar someone had given me had a bundle of miniature doves in it, doves I needed to let loose. So I busted the sand dollar on the porch roof outside my bedroom window and sprinkled the tiny white pieces onto the shingles and did not sleep. That night, the rain washed them off into the iris bed below; I found them the next morning. Even as a twenty-year-old, I was giddy at the airport—flying for the first time and proud of how adept I was with the electronic kiosk. Mom had driven me there, her face full of question. I slid my credit card through and punched in my passport number, eager to find my gate and take off.

I wasn't an unhappy kid; it just always seemed that *up* was the preferred direction in which to go. Maybe my granddad's admonition convinced me that the life lived, especially the rough or shameful or disappointing parts, was something to fly from—we are always to rise, above the dirt-poor houses of our fathers in a family of thirteen kids, above the splitting shoes and homemade blouses of our mothers, above a life of obscurity. Above the mountains that fold in too close.

The paperback *Cloud of Unknowing* sits beside me in the passenger seat, with its goofy Seventies cover. I'm wondering: if I strike and stick with it, come hell or whatever, would the cloud all but dissipate so that I'm face to face with God? With whatever is most true? But I need to read on to find that out. For now, I leave the book closed. I figure, though, that if I were to strike with my sharp dart, with my longing love, and let the dread creep in like cold, then I might have to let go of my preference for escape.

***

I fingered the cat's eye marbles in my pocket. As it neared evening, the supper dishes clinked in the dining hall sinks. The women began their hum back and forth to the kitchen, Betty giving orders. The men leaned back on the folding chairs so their stomachs ballooned out big; they clasped their hands there on their bellies and put in a chew of tobacco or a rub of Copenhagen snuff. The time was right, and I slipped out of my chair and joined my jittery cousins at the edge of the baseball field where the helicopter sat.

Harry came out soon enough and started it up. The black blade turned, slow at first, and then it whirred into nothing. He started taking us up in twos and threes. All of our scrawny bodies pulsed for the front of the line at the fence near the batter's box. As I stood waiting, a tall, wide shape moved up beside me. It was the cousin whom I'd noticed earlier in the rush of cousins beside the dining hall. His arms weren't bouncing at his sides now. His shaggy black hair sprawled and gave way before the force of the blade's wind. His eyes were glassed over yet full of force, and he held his mouth open in a pout as though speech were about to come, but it didn't.

The boy wore baggy jeans and a big white T-shirt with a stretched neckline. He was enormous, probably three hundred pounds, and he looked about seventeen. I still knew only a couple of my second cousins' names, and I wondered who he was and whose he was—he might have been Aunt Susie's boy, or Gail and Mike's. He was big like Mike.

I remembered the story of the older cousin who had gone after his own sister with scissors, and for a moment I feared it was him. But then the boy looked down at me with a face somehow like a baby's and, saying nothing, he reached for me and hugged me with his doughy arms. He held me a little too long, smothering my face in his T-shirt, but I wasn't all that afraid; I sensed no intent to harm. He released me after I squirmed a little, and I smoothed my hair and we both went back to waiting as Uncle Harry escorted a few boys back from their ride. My cousin looked down at me once more, then all at once lunged forward past the line of eager kids and met Uncle Harry near the second base marker, midway between the crowd of kids and the helicopter.

His excitement rippled through his body, and some of my girl cousins giggled. He and Harry stood there in a kind of dance. Then Harry shook his head, said something into the boy's ear and slapped him once on the back. Then, as if told a goldmine secret, the giant boy turned from Harry, smiling big, and strode back toward us.

He's going the wrong way, I thought. But his eyes shone. He looked so ready to steal away into the sky, because isn't that what he and I and everyone were supposed to want? To lift off and leave Spencer and its muggy nights behind, to shake it off like a damned June bug?

The boy looked right at me.

"I'm too fat!" he blurted with his hands raised up like thick wings. "Uncle Harry says there's a weight limit and I might crash it." He laughed a little, crossed his arms and turned to watch as four others bolted for the helicopter door. My cousin Nathan took my hand and jerked me forward. I nearly left the ground when he pulled me, weightless, like one of Betty's nylon slips on the wash line. I was in a half-trot toward the machine, straining to look back over my shoulder for that beaming sweaty face, an anchored body in a white tee. Uncle Harry was at the door then; he grabbed me and lifted me into the helicopter before I could turn back around and say, "Let me stay, leave me be." Twenty of my little selves could've fit in there. I was wedged in between two punchy twins and felt my belly drop down into my toes as we lifted.

I started to cry, but no one paid attention. I felt like I might throw up; I covered my face with one hand and reached for the cat's eye marbles in my pocket with the other, just so I could touch them. But, as the electrified, drawled voices around me grew hushed and then went silent, I spread my fingers from my eyes, then slid my hand away entirely and looked down.

Through the glass floor of the helicopter, past my canvas shoes, a tin-roofed dollhouse must have been the dining hall, with a porch I couldn't quite make out, a porch that I knew had screen around it keeping the bugs off the grownups as they gathered out there in the late light. The cluster of kids at the fence shrank to an anthill, just like Harry had said they would. The whole 4-H camp turned into a green blanket with play things on it, trees into little pom-poms, the road a dirty frayed ribbon. It seemed that we might fly northward, over my house on the hillside, and would I be able to recognize it when I saw it, or tell Mom when I saw her that the house all but disappeared inside the mountain, or when would I even see her again? All was disappearing as we kept going up, and I found myself pressing my face closer and closer to the glass floor, straining to make out shapes and buildings—where was the boy who had held me?

It was my first flight, my first leaving, and I sobbed for the boy left behind; I still felt his fleshy arms enveloping me in a smother. I wept at how empty and how wonderful it was to rise, at how horribly I loved leaving. At how I longed for what I'd left.

***

The Cloud is pinched under my arm as I get milk from the refrigerator and put my Jiffy Lube receipt under a magnet on the fridge door. I sip the milk in the kitchen, and it comes clear to me just what has troubled and excited me about these words: *Strike with the sharp dart of longing love—and do not leave it no matter what happens.* They reveal my contradictions, the schism in myself. I know the anonymous author meant for his or her words to keep to the context of mystical union with God, but the words loose a spout in me and I cannot help but let the contradictions spill forth: my unsteadying pangs of homesickness, and my fierce insistence on leaving home; my ache for the sound of a slack screen door shutting after my mother's heels, and the thrill of having gone off to school and finding work, work of my own; my resolution to be okay with being nothing, as existentially calm as a doe, and my white-hot fear of not having accomplished anything impressive before the reckoning comes. My regret for having betrayed what I have loved, and my coming to see this betrayal as something at the core of what makes us human.

In the kitchen, I feel that sting of my own betrayal, and I return to my five-year-old self, in a flimsy body, on the helicopter ride at the Boggs Reunion of 1984 when my too-big cousin stood by and watched from his place beside the batter's box. I return to that day when it wasn't yet betrayal that I felt, only an incoherent ache. Embodied contradiction without understanding; just two big feelings at once: exultation and despair.

I suppose when my helicopter ride was over and Harry landed, it would've been near dark. My cousins would have been begging for just one more ride, and the boy left behind would have still been standing there, nearly a silhouette, and I shy before him. But, try as I may, I can't remember when we came down. I don't remember coming back, and I don't remember ever seeing the boy again. There is no clear ending.

So I'll end it, this time, by staying where my longing strikes. I stay with the dread felt in a small self. I stay with the boy, where the mountains fold in on themselves. He is anchored. I do him no favor by staying, I just bury my face in his white T-shirt. It's like a bed sheet, and I smell the musty dog days of Spencer and the flecks of Copenhagen the boy had dropped when he'd dipped with one of the men. I stay for the length of the evening, at least.

Reliable Outcome | *The Figure*

Why did you give us
such tender skin
and ask us
to carry fire?

—Jan Richardson

On a broken day of my thirty-third year, we look at the worksheets on prime factorization. The two adolescent girls, Miriam and Doriana, have a math test tomorrow. The factor trees, pretty and neat in the example problems, branch down like Christmas trees: a number, let's say forty-two, with a skirt of two, three, seven, indivisible. An unprepared tutor, I have come carrying nothing, so one of the girls pulls a nub of pencil from her pack, tears me out some scratch paper. I try to remember my own young self, to inhabit her again and learn anew how to get inside to the inner workings of a number—to find a way to explain—it's like living inside a big clock and touching the gears, knowing them in the dark, the smallest pieces, and, from then on, for the rest of life, working from memory. Soon: tongue-tip out the corner of the mouth, the hallmark of childlike concentration. The trusted steps of arithmetic, the smells of adolescence, the poor basement light that is cool light—we work.

The next page is "Find the Greatest Common Factor." We are to find the so-called greatest common factor between, let's say, fifty-four and thirty. More trees, and do you see how we circle the common factors in both trees, as if catching them in a butterfly net? *Common* means *shared*, I say over and over when they swipe their pencil-line nets to catch uncommon factors, rogues, and then erase and leave phantom errors in the trees, forgotten tinsel. Let's think of the common factors between us: arms, legs, loss, hair, teeth, barrettes (though mine does not have a crocheted flower with a button at the center), eyeballs, underarm hair shaved down to dots, memory (though mine is wider and more fractured), girlhood (though theirs is steaming). And the greatest common factor? Well—what I want to tell them is that math is a sensible thing, like a dress with pockets, for there will be days when sensible will be preferred over meaningful, when they will get up and dress in the morning because it is the sensible thing even when all is meaningless and the heart is a crash of hard edges, and I want to say that, although your test is tomorrow and your mothers are mad about your lousy grades, this factoring skill will not be helpful to you in life when you do your taxes or look for work or try sex, when you find your life a wreckage, but it will be a skill you might return to simply for its reliable outcome because, aside from the larger primes, you can always break down a number by a factor of two, or try three, there is always a place to begin. And, well, I'd say the greatest common factor between us is our skin, burnable, our skin that can touch and sense the hexagon of the pencils we trade, skin that contains our souls like a sack, and so much will be required of you, of me, of our skin as it must brush up against the world.

But it is spring and our hour is over. I return the borrowed pencil, and I see, spread over the table, sheets and sheets of trees made of scribbled numbers, a forest, and all at once I sense someone running, a figure rushing toward us, from out of the trees, with arms stretched out, coming to us—apron, headscarf, faceless but somehow it's a familiar face, someone always dwelling there, waiting, among the solid and simpler numbers, with skin on fire but she's not afraid, rushing from the trees toward the three of us, through the branches snagging her skirt, headlong through our errors, the erased pencil lines, as if through harmless cobwebs, arms out—but then the girls gather up their scrap paper and jam it into their packs because it is spring and it is time to go and they have their lives to rush into.

Litany for the Body | *C.P.*

Goldenrod at its peak looks like it's dying in the late light of October. Still, I rivet my eyes as I pull off to the shoulder and take in the great swath of it along Route 219. I'm driving home from a wedding, full of pulled pork and slaw and the hope that the couple makes it. The engine idles, I sit swollen with the rare desire to extend the day, the way, as kids in cutoffs, we put a ghostman on third so we could keep playing after the neighbors and cousins went home and there weren't enough bodies for teams. The broken seat of a swing—home plate, the lilac bush—first base, the stone slab marking where the septic tank was buried—second, and there at the apple tree—on third—we could see the shape of the ghost, holding the branch, poised to be hit home. From somewhere, a mother called in our grass-stained bodies, blurring us into one body that shimmered. Maybe because of the wedding, and because of the sorry goldenrod, the full, aging gust of it off the berm, because its whole is more achingly beautiful than the sum of its parts, my discrete self that was barreling south on 219 is all at once aware that she is not discrete at all. Of course, none of us are, but we try to maintain that illusion of separateness. I could cut the engine, spill out into the gold and the few spikes of ironweed and tufted thistle, and crack open to know my life keenly as something that is not mine.

What is it I am remembering? It is my hard little body I had thought a chiseled thing set apart, rocketing around, and then the thrill of that other October evening cooling, our fingers difficult to bend, so cold, as the dark lay its blanket of chill around the church, the door gaping open to the church yard, the larger body I realized I belonged to and could not leave behind. And could not save.

I am, again, twelve, lifting up the tea towel and sneaking two warm oatmeal cookies for myself. Wide gooey discs my mother has baked for the Beatty youth choir. I cup the crumbs that tear loose from the edges. I am home from school, solemnly delivered by the school bus with its interior air all skidded up with Mötley Crüe, the Helmick boy's tape that no one really heard. The school day has been a haze, sixth grade containing our bodies lined up for lunch, my ear attuned to shoes clicking on the hard floor, each little tick definite and startling.

C.P. has died, the boy in the youth choir's back row.

C.P.'s voice was bread dough, so soft, worked over, and rising. It was as if we all heard the sighing-down when he died in the wreck this morning. As if we could feel his body walking back to the fogged road out of a truck coiled around a tree, with not a scratch on him, then his heart snapping loose as he folded to the ground like a pillowcase doll. We are all patting our bodies to make sure they're still here, awareness acute all over: each of my underarm hairs like a tuber's growing eye, spreading out to feel and feel, I pull at them. My training bra crosses my chest like a harness, my eyes sting and my lips pucker out as if punched. The two cookies are gone and I lie back on my blue gingham bedspread wishing I hadn't stolen them. Wishing I could eat all the rest.

But could I feel him fall over like a pillowcase doll? No, maybe not that. I couldn't feel the no-more of breath or heartbeat. It's everyone else I felt and I feel, the ones left, it's as if they are swelling my body, as if I have only dreamt them before now, back when I thought they were separate from me.

In the morning, after we heard C.P. had died, we dressed by the fire. I did not think: This is a day to mark, a time-mark inked into my diary. Still. My brothers and my sister and I rose in the dark, knocked against one another like pups. We pressed palms to the heat of the fireplace and stood in our night clothes with our jeans hung over a chair back, inside-out, so they would warm our legs, our bones. Over my head, I pulled on my brother Jake's high school sweatshirt, without asking if I could wear it. Central Preston arched in blocky orange letters on the front, his football number on the back. We watched for stray cinders, sat at the table for our bowls of Cream of Wheat and cinnamon toast made from leftover biscuits. When my sister went to hairspray her big hair, I saw that some cold Cream of Wheat still coated the bottom of her bowl, the grainy white she had sweetened. When no one was looking, I ate what she had left.

C.P. had a wide-moon face like my sister's. He teased me from the back row of the choir. He promised me that, when I got older, I would be his girl and wear his jacket. I did not find him handsome, but I rehearsed it in my mind, imagined myself with his high school jacket on, the orange *Central Preston* on the fake leather that would make static with my rayon blouse, one of Diane Annette's castoffs. I would have worn the jacket down the halls at school, listening to the pleasing click of my short jelly shoe heels on the floor, and down the aisle of the school bus in the morning when I boarded and watched my mother's shape in the doorway of the house through the windows, in her black barn sweater. I would have worn his jacket in the churchyard with the other girls, talking over what flowers—gladiolas maybe—for my wedding up in the grove across from Beatty Church, under the pavilion. I would have stroked the single line of snaps down the front, rehearsing the nearness of his last name to my first, over and over.

We four huddled in prayer with Mom, holding hands, bearing backpacks, Mom had pinto beans on a low boil for a faraway supper. Then I ran for the bus with the other three, sensing more than seeing the firebrands of the tulip poplars and the maples shrill with sugar and the goldenrod sagging at the fence line. Running, I felt how present C.P. was in his absence, as if he were running with us, our ghostman hit home. I could feel his jacket on me instead of Jake's sweatshirt. The air was wet on my face as I ran. I thought how this was a place of tucked-back houses with long gravel drives, I thought of when we had gone to Gaye's house where she'd taken in her mom until she'd died, and the house smelled of that camphor, the small scoop puckered the blanket and a depression held on the thin pillow with a barn scene on it. Leaving Gaye's in the night, we had waited for one of my brothers to unlatch the cattle gate at the end of the drive, and a black angus rubbed the car door with its hot nose, benign but ghostly—or did it? Did we find the smudge? Did we only sense the shape, black out of the black? And now C.P.'s soft body so present, we all watched for it out the bus windows, to show up between us and Mom silhouetted and still standing there as Willie shifted gears and chugged on.

After supper's pinto beans with ketchup, cornbread, onions, of which I have eaten little because of the two cookies, we head the mile and a half to Beatty for choir practice. It is not yet cold, but it will be. We crest the hill and jostle down the rutted grove road to the small white church with its outhouse in back, curtained by white lattice. There is the broken-down school bus, hood up, at the edge of the lot, there's the dog that runs his line out beyond the church's fence, toward and away from the Wilsons' huddle of buildings growing like tumors off the trailer. We cut through the grove, past its pavilion and the water pump standing sentinel.

Inside, we situate ourselves on the wooden chairs and Mom leaves the door gaping open, behind the pulpit, framing the dusk-glory of fall and leading out to mossy concrete stairs and the path to the outhouse. The choir is three Opels, two Dodge girls, my two brothers and my sister Miss and me, the Molissee boys but only sometimes and not today, Gaye's granddaughters Karen and Diane Annette who give Miss and me their blouses when they're through with them, and their cousin Tom who acts up and tries to sing bass with my brothers. The scent of lemon Pledge hangs over the polished altar.

Mom plays the tenor part four times because Matthew Opel is tone-deaf and can't pick it out when she plays all the harmony parts together. C.P. was the other tenor, he sang worse than Matthew, they guessed at the tenor notes from the back row. Now untethered, Matthew sits by me, in the front where I sing soprano. The dusk thickens and promises to be pure by the time we quit our songs and Matthew's leg warms mine. Slowly we feel ourselves flaming as the inside of Beatty becomes the only thing bright in the falling dark. Mom gives Diane the soprano solo about the blind man now seeing, Verse Three, because we all know her voice is best, but it hurts me anyway. "Here I Am, Lord," "When You Walk Through a Storm," "Come Unto Me." We keep singing, sounding no better than when we started, but we know what will happen when we stop, when we acknowledge the chill setting in, our fingers bone-cold, our young tender nipples alert under our shirts and bras. We understand the smallness of our band now smaller, in this space lit up against the night, and when we spill out of here, grabbing cookies from the tin on the way, we will hunt fearfully for each other by sound and touch as we stray into the darkness, away from the church-window squares of light.

Some of the songs are from the shape-note book, some from the big red hymnal, most from photocopied sheets Mom got from somewhere, but they all become one litany, and it seems that they have always been that, our entreaties, not only for C.P. who walked out of the truck wreckage and walked no farther, whom we could not save, but also for the people of this small place dying out, the Beatty people who have formed our first intuitions of love. Entreaty also for ourselves, for each other, our blood pulsing with time. We cannot save ourselves either. Our raspy songs grow big with feelings too much for us, they forecast into the future, to a time when our ghosts will outnumber us.

So we sing a litany for the body we are part of. It could be something mystical, how people talk about the body of God, of Christ. I don't know about that. I know only that this is where I learn I am not my own and that I'll never leave this place, this tiny pocket of West Virginia. None of us will, even when we do leave, for college and the Marines and Philadelphia and New Jersey, for marriage, for divorce, for tree-trimming in Atlanta making better money than we can make here. We sing our litany for eyes watching the dark that is only dark until you look harder—then it takes the shape of the water pump rising out of the ground.

For the mouth of the Wilsons' broken-down school bus yielding its engine to the wild grape.

For Mary Jane's tumor, her lost leg, her chained half-mad husky, her long gravel drive lost to the pines.

For Matthew's hand I could take, but don't.

For legs too naked without runner-free nylons so Cindy misses on Sunday and we inquire—Home sick, her girls say and we let it be.

For the head heavy upon the pillow with a barn on it, the bear pressing its bulk into the leaf pile in the grove—Bob saw it and told us, C.P.'s father, Bob's voice is like bread dough, worked over, and rising.

For Jean who drinks.

For the bulbous head of the gladiola in the ground, dormant and then—and Mr. Bell who lets his gladiolas go haywire after Pat dies.

For toes rubbed raw by the jelly shoe.

For Harold who brings books and wool caps and bits of used Dial soap from the Tucker County Boys' Home for my brothers and sister and me, and goes blind.

For the body that wears polyester, has a mess of knots for hands, eats buckwheat cakes soured from twenty-year-old starter kept on the sill, for the body that limps.

For the eyes sprouting on the potatoes in the dank bin in the cellar.

For the frilled face of the strong gladiolas—I will still choose gladiolas. I will always choose them.

For the dried locust feet, hair-thin but clinging to the church siding until we flick them off and the casings crush.

For Jean's arthritic hands spanking Miss when she climbed all over the altar because she didn't see it as any holier than a plank of fence.

For the mouth gulping their weeping, some of it, all of it.

For fingers on the banjo strings and untuned piano and rough moustache and stray wisps of hair.

For C.P.'s moon-face like Miss's like Mom's, and for Miss's torso fitting the denim jumper from Diane Annette from Karen from Connie from Trudy from—

And we do rush out, in time, we grab our cookies from the tin on the front pew and run out to find the locusts and the chestnut burrs. We cannot sing forever. We are natives to the light racing out into the tar black where there is, waiting, the dead bus ghost, the water pump unyielding, the world of billions of people whose lives are fiercely extraordinary and bound up with ours, since Beatty is but our foretaste. The litany moves into our pumping arms and legs running, a litany that never stops in the great October world.

I sneak back into the church where Mom gathers her song sheets and grieves. I come back in to seek Mom and her perm and ragged-sad face and jeans and homemade blouse, she is not old. *Come here*, she says without turning to look at me, and she grabs me and holds me. I guess I want to say I stole the cookies, and I wish she'd given me the solo. I want to say I can't love this place and this people enough. They are strangers to me, they are mirrors of me, and I can't escape them but I long to, and I'm sorry. I wish I could own my life and this hard little body and be shed of the larger one that will demand too much. But she and I can't say anything at all, we can only crack open.

Work Ethic | *Leah*

Now Laban had two daughters. The name of the older was Leah, and the name of the younger was Rachel...So Jacob served seven years for Rachel, and they seemed to him but a few days because of the love he had for her...Laban gathered together all the people of the place and made a feast. But in the evening he took his daughter Leah and brought her to Jacob, and he went in to her...And in the morning, behold, it was Leah! And Jacob said to Laban, "What is this you have done to me? Did I not serve with you for Rachel? Why then have you deceived me?" Laban said, "It is not so done in our country, to give the younger before the firstborn. Complete the week of this one, and we will give you the other also in return for serving me another seven years." Jacob did so, and completed her week. Then Laban gave him his daughter Rachel to be his wife...So Jacob went in to Rachel also, and he loved Rachel more than Leah.

—Genesis 29.16-20

What I think is that she wakes up one morning and clears it all out. The men are counting their toes and their new sons' toes, their umpteen wives, their purses of coin, scooping their barley heads into mounds like boys with contraband raisins. They flick the flies away, sneak watch chains under their coats, and the big heads of their hundred cattle rise and follow the trail of the sun with their velvet noses.

It's no wonder it's a man—it's Jacob—that dreams the ladder with restless angels clambering up and down, unable to decide between heaven and earth, because there are piles of good things everywhere— it's distracting. And the women tally theirs too, even though their piles are smaller: a bracelet and gourd dipper, jug of clean water, a marriage which means a tent over your head. But I think that one day Leah clears out the place and walks up out of there, all the people watching this woman married by custom, the eldest daughter first before the younger one that Jacob really wanted. The people have always thought Leah mad for his favor, that because she is daily unloved by a husband who will open her legs only in pitch dark, and call her by her sister's name, Rachel, his other wife, that she is to be pitied. But that is not what I think, not anymore. I think she is mad for something else. I think she has always gone about her regions of work in search of the main region: she went ahead and found names for her baby boys, she named them See, Hear, Fasten, Praise, and the later ones Hire and Dwell—her only girl she named Judgment—then she went on with the wash, the mopping, the beating of rugs, the tabulation of Jacob's coins, all the while keeping all her old selves straight, on a string of beads, which I know to be a lot of work.

Loving him hasn't been work, not really, not with his beautiful black hair and slight lisp, but she can't be bothered with even that task today. No, today she gets down to the main work of clearing out the cluttering good of these comfortable things, the extra baggage, the clothes on her back, water in the well, her station in the tent village as a woman of means, whether pitied or not. She woke up this morning nearly smothered by these things that wear out her heart which is trying to see through them, like a kid in a crowd at the dogfights, hearing the terror of the gnawed shank but not getting to see it—go on and clear the crowd. I think she is naked and climbing the ridge beyond the swamp, climbing all morning and evening, into the night, her princely boys left sleeping, rocked by the handmaid, and Judgment with her hair a tangled spray on the pillow, and Leah stands out there, smelling peat moss and spruce, in the dark. She can breathe out there, terrified by so uncrowded a place, knowing, yes, this should terrify her. She vows right now to climb back down and work so hard to tell them there is something beyond all that, to tell the men hoarding their barley mounds, the women vying for new dresses and his favor and a son with the best name—to tell them (*tell me*) that you must come up here, out beyond the tents, where it is bare and lonely and shaped like loss. Otherwise how will you ever know your unknown self, a bead neither lost nor found, not a bead at all? How will you ever know, for the very first time, what it is you have always wanted?

The Long Weeping | *Rizpah*

for JL

That wasn't supposed to happen, but then,
What is?
So now the night is part of everything.

—James Galvin, "Putting Down the Night"

The king took the two sons of Rizpah, daughter of Aiah, whom
she bore to Saul…and the five sons of Merab, daughter of Saul…
He gave them into the hands of the Gibeonites, and they impaled
them on the mountain before the Lord. The seven of them per-
ished together. They were put to death in the first days of harvest,
at the beginning of the barley harvest. Then Rizpah, the daughter
of Aiah, took sackcloth and spread it on a rock for herself, from
the beginning of harvest until rain fell on them from the heavens;
she did not allow the birds of the air to come on the bodies by day,
or the wild animals by night.

—2 Samuel 21.8-10

She throws rocks at pigeons and songbirds alike. The woman is not
magnanimous, no, not even toward the childless milky girl who comes
and sits with her and brings her those flavored potato chips, jalapeño,
because the woman can't handle Kroger anymore.

Under her jalapeño breath: *Maybe some nectarines next time.* But
then the woman takes it back, *Never mind*, like she always does, because

of what worth is the sluicing of fruit in the mouth without a sense of smell? It all tastes like kitchen sponges.

The milky girl who unmade her floursack doll for the woman's horrible flag that she waves at buzzards and hyenas and the snapping teeth of the fox says, *What about dried bananas?*

The woman, Rizpah, the one with corded-weed hair and only the ratty suggestion of a dress on her body, nicks a swallow's beak with a stone she throws. *What about them? What could you know—you still have your milk teeth.*

Rizpah is all out of ideas. She turns back to the seven bodies hanging in the trees. This time, she looks at the foot of the youngest dangling dead boy. Toes scuff the rock beneath: if toes were fingers they'd be drawing with sidewalk chalk. Rizpah has had to agree to the terms of the blue shadows. She doesn't know how long this will take, this sitting here among large and small stones eating the stale snacks the tiresome sweet girl brings her. She knows only the snow's rising drifts, no, the desert sand's drifts—there is of course no snow here—and the birds' skimming-over and the foxes' brushing-against and the contours of the bodies in darkness, in light, in darkness, in light, and their leaden movement when the wind moves them.

The Beginning

Rizpah hid her car in the woods and chose a smooth rock to sit on by the thin river. It was in the first days of the barley harvest and the dry ground hissed at her ankles. Nearby, the seven boys, impaled, hung like ornaments from the trees because there had been a famine for three years and young King David had inquired of God in the voice that a king uses, *Why are we starving, O God, why won't it rain,* and God had answered in a voice disguised and muffled like a prank caller's: *Because of the sins on the old king's head—Saul left a price unpaid when he died.* And so David paid it, eagerly, with the currency common among kings: with the dead bodies of Saul's seven heirs to the throne David now sat upon.

Rizpah was Saul's surviving concubine, a no-wife, then, when Saul died, less than a widow, and now a no-mother: two of the boys her sons, five her grandsons. It's a tale of kings—Saul's fresh bones were still rattling for rectitude and burial while David, just a boy really, preened, had the royal robes hemmed and fitted—and in the margins, as with any tale, are scribbled the unanswered questions. One was the question of the concubine, the royal rape, for who knows whether her body was hijacked or not, whether, as a girl of fifteen, she had welcomed Saul's touch or not? Let's say the smudged marginalia suggest no, she did not welcome it, and the only God she believed was the God who knows what it's like to have arms stretched back, to be done to and not doing. *God knows that or God knows nothing,* she said, and she birthed boys whom she watched play in the cattails, and they made her bracelets of violets and twist-ties and licorice and grass. In the tale of kings, God looked on approvingly as the stakes went through each boy's body (she smelled something sharp, like limes, when the first body broke, then she smelled nothing at all and has smelled nothing since). But that is the tale Rizpah knew better than to believe. She chose a smooth rock by the river knowing King David had put words in God's mouth because

God had no words. *God has stones in the mouth or God has nothing.*

She took a cloth of black goat hair, spread it with care on the rock, as if laying a tablecloth patterned with tulips. Then she had to decide what to do there. She sat and sat. Was she angry? She did not know. Was she dead? She did not think so. She sniffed at a handful of pine needles: nothing. So she really had lost her sense of smell, though she could see, could hear, keenly. She knew she would get mean and lowdown. She feared she would go crazy. But there was also a softness, dangerous, gossamer, and she muttered about that, tried to brush it from her exposed arms as if brushing off dust left from moths. The turkey vultures came to the corpses to survey, and at first she swatted and spit because their heads were so ugly and offensive, their feet hideous. But when they came again, and, with them, a sniffing hyena casting more than one blue shadow, she knew, without thinking, what she would do.

She weaved dead reeds and sticks, strips of her sleeve, some hair ribbons, some ropey strands of tire littered from the highway bridge above her (and eventually the remnants of the girl's floursack doll), into a flag and flapped it standing by her rock. She would keep watch and wave the beasts away, as though the boys were only sleeping and she had only to shoo the flies from their faces so they would not wake from their afternoon nap. That is what she would do. It was not an idea, but simply what her body decided.

How could she know that it would take seven months, that it would take until the end of the worrisome barley harvest? And that after those seven months, David, the boy king, having wrung his hands watching her demented vigil (*Necrophiliac*, some spitefully whispered; *Saint*, others said, *but batty as hell*), would finally honor Saul's bones, parade them through the streets in a gaudy pearlescent box—such bravado—and bury them, and bury, too, the ashy bones of the seven brittle boy bodies untouched by the teeth of beasts? And that, then, with the sins paid for and the royal bones rightly honored, the boy king's God, supposedly appeased, would send the rain? How could it be that, after all that, David would sulk down to her river rock and want to marry her, this Rizpah in rags who stood sentinel for the bodies dead by his hand, and that holy men would praise her acts that instructed the too-ignorant but beloved boyish king?

She knows none of this in these early days when the barley is coming into pitiful head. And, even after this tale will all come to pass, it will not matter: it will remain a tale of kings exalting a God of kings, and the bits of praise leftover for her she will wipe from her eyes, like crusts of sleep.

Because there is another tale and another God, one who does not grant, does not bargain in blood, does not withhold or send rain: just aches from inside Rizpah's horsehoof mouth, her chipped teeth, her slackened jaw that can't comprehend fruit.

Where can I find God, she asked herself the first night on the smooth rock on the goat-hair rug, as her legs went numb. *In Hell of course*, the answer came, but from where? Who knows. *In this stand of trees where boyflesh is going nowhere but to yellowblack and pus. God takes to the trees of Hell.* The only Psalm she remembered, a Psalm of David that he wrote as a pensive little boy but soon forgot—it slipped through his ringed fingers—says of God, *If I make my bed in Sheol, behold you are there.*

So here you are, she said, adding a candy bar wrapper to her weave of flag. *You are in Hell or you are nowhere, and the shadows are bruising us both blue.*

And so she sits here—her body narrow and compact with no room for ideas—and she flaps her horrible flag to keep at bay the teeth and teeth and beak that snap at the bodies of the boys impaled between the lungs and hung. Rizpah like an electric wire downed by a storm, for seven months. And what of her longing for fruit? Her sense of smell? Her disfigurement as her appendages and organs fall off one by one (the first, in the cold Kroger dairy aisle), refusing the greater pain of holding memory? What of her unoiled weedy hair? What of her sex, her stolen wild animal body? What of the random girl who sneaks her food and fusses with Rizpah's natty hair? What of the many who pass and call out or don't, or speed by on motorbikes? What of her skin tanned to rough hide, then to diaphanous wing?

Deafness

After her first few mutterings, Rizpah said nothing at all for the first month, no words, not even to the milky girl in the grocery-clerk smock when, out of nowhere, she brought her unraveled doll to add to the flag (they would talk later, but theirs was a silent exchange early on). Rizpah flapped the flag at hyenas and fox teeth, at the sickly bear and the daytime ravens with voices that sounded like a belly tearing open. She hated the ravens almost as much as the cocky pigeons. The wind was hot and it played with the bodies, moving the branches they hung from: marionettes, this way and that. When the boys' faces turned from her, she got up from her rock and walked until they faced her again. She was invisibly tied to the corpses, never walking out beyond a certain radius. Back and forth, in an arc, or in a hoop, like a donkey grinding grain with its revolutions, harnessed as it is. There was nowhere to go. Except to have their faces facing hers again. One day the wind grew wilder and blew the bodies in a spin: large horrible whirligigs. And she finally spoke, and sternly: *Don't turn from me, look at me,* but of course it was the wind's fault, not theirs. She said it as though scolding them, and it would be the only time she would speak to them directly—mother to sons—for she saw that they spun and spun, deaf. After that, something gave and she spoke freely and often and loudly and softly. Not to the boys. She just talked. There was a strange gift in it. She did not speak out of any role or assigned part, as she had all her life, fawning after her father, or after the king, or after the toddling boys. She was still hitched, yes, tracing that arc back and forth to find their faces when the wind turned them, but her words were unhitched and unyielding, unhitched even to logic or reverence or fear or regret. *You can say anything here,* she said to herself, *because all the hearers are dead.*

Things She Did Not Expect

Tree frogs. Fruit's absence having its own shape. The thirst beneath thirst and the pink skin beneath that. Something about the dew. The boys' wounds not scabbing over. The feeling of sadness in her teeth and the sickliness of the poor bear. The brittle fortitude beneath the silence beneath the maggoted wing of the turkey vulture, its barnacled face. That there was always a beneath, a *before*, even when memory shut its doors. That there was always a cellophane-wrapped snack cake left by the girl.

The blood beneath her on the rock, and no tampons. That her monthly blood would keep happening at all and her legs would fall asleep. Boredom. The easy lift of her eyelids. The ache to be touched and the dark light in herself, clitoral. (How long since? She cannot say how long.) That there could be light with no evidence of light. That the boredom could sometimes surpass the grief. That even when the air felt like powder, she still could not smell the powder, or anything at all. She did not expect tree frogs singing their unhidden song from their very hidden places. And there was no expectation that she would not go crazy. (So did she?) She did not expect the way the tree frogs climbed the night with a green joy that complicated things, made her feel guilty—a sudden irrevocable joy, like an assault. She did not expect that someone would bring her a hot towel coiled into the shape of a rose and that her skin could sigh, her very skin.

Before the Beginning: The Stagecoach Motel

Rizpah drove for hours after the executions, semi-blind, unable to read any road signs, so of course she just went in circles on the beltway and ended up near home, but couldn't go home, so she checked into the Stagecoach Motel. She didn't know then where they'd hung the bodies: she would discover them. She would find them hanging, impossibly, when she would go for a walk by the river looking for a lynx that night.

They had HBO at the Stagecoach Motel, and she got very drunk watching this special on the lynx and so she thought she would go out and see herself a lynx by the river, a majestic animal with pointy tufts of black on its ears, with paws crossed in front of it or stretched into a long leap, and she knew it would be missing an ear (chewed off) and would have the all-around mangy look of the sound of stray cats because she'd just taken a bath with the window cracked open and had heard them in back of the motel, their strangled feral cries, and she was just about to go under and hold herself there, drown herself in the tub because she'd looked in the mirror and couldn't see her face, semi-blind as she was. She was there in the tub tracing the nice straight grouting between the tiles, about to drown herself, but (drunk already) it felt as if she'd be drowning those damned stray cats with chewed ears, so she rose up, wrapped in a dress, had a plastic cup more of Chianti, and watched the nature channel with lynx cubs and lynx summer naps and lynx circling the feeble antelope young, and then she went down to the dirty river to see herself a lynx with a missing ear, a cross between a circling lynx and a mewling stray. But no moon and no lynx, only a few geese and some panties strung up in the trees like tinsel, some trash in the river foam. Then, vision still blurry, she thought she saw a heron, a great blue, all spidery legs and whooshy wings (she doesn't know birds, but she knows geese and heron, pigeon and swallow, and some that sing), but no, when she got close she saw that it was a busted outboard motor, then she saw them.

The seven bodies.

Vision razor sharp, all at once. She picked over the rocks and cans in her slippers (was she even wearing slippers?), studying the heavy hanging bodies as if they were an art piece. Her mouth was full of stones, but the stones were wine-soaked kitchen sponges—drunk-slur—and the droughted river, in the background, made a sound with its flow that was hardly a sound. Time mixed with time, and it was not long or short or bearable or unbearable: it simply passed and she wasn't sure anymore how much there was of it. She was ancient, eternal, a figment of the future, a blip—she was not yet born.

She slept on a not-so-comfortable rock (which is why, later, she would choose a nice smooth one). She woke up hungover and felt as if someone were giving her life back to her, like a cold potato she didn't want to eat the first time, or the second time, or the third. She woke to a cold-potato morning, shoved it away again, got up, and went back to the Stagecoach, looked stupidly at the Classifieds on the dresser. Secretarial. She called a place without thinking, for she couldn't think, she asked for a job interview (still sponge-mouthed, and—there in the back of her mind—the bodies were drifting to the left slightly, to the right with a gust). She pressed her beige suit and swiffed her hair (exquisite then, not weedy at all) and decided to go down to the river once more before the interview, still in her slippers.

A college rowing team skated by like a silent water bug, and they didn't seem to see her—so was she really there? She wasn't sure, but she liked them, their silent motion, their arms all figured out and performing. They didn't speak, the rowers, so she waved uselessly. She brushed down her beige skirt and sat on another sharp rock. A goose came close; she threw a rock at it, then threw it a peppermint from her purse. Out of the corner of her eye: the wind slow-spun the corpses just a little. She tried to remember how fast she could type, how few the errors.

She saw the wide smooth rock, like a bed, like a bier. She saw without thinking. Okay, she said, as if offered something to be agreed to, like a job. She trudged back to the Stagecoach in her slippers to undress and put on the wrap dress, a lovely kind of kimono, from the night before. One more swiff of her hair, then goodbye to it all. She left her other dresses hanging in the closet, taking only the goat-hair weave, and, returning to the riverside, she chose the smooth rock, not yet knowing what she would do there. She put down the goat-hair: tossed it up, hands at two corners, and let it fall so lightly into place, like a tablecloth.

Why She Can't Handle Kroger Anymore: Before the Before

Before she drove and drove in circles—semi-blind, white-eyed—and checked into the Stagecoach Motel that night, Rizpah pulled into the Kroger parking lot and fumbled toward its eternal fluorescence. She stared at the carts in which baby boys could sit at the front and dangle their legs, she grabbed a basket instead and roamed the aisles. She got some looks when she toppled the display of Keebler cookies. There was no rational sensation in her *just the sensation that I set fire to my own curtains and the whole house went up, and isn't my face now burned and disfigured and all the horrible scarring in place now,* and she touched her cheek to see. *What home? Set fire to what home? What surrounds me now? No wall of the citadel, no place in the reeds where they played.* She sniffed at the mangoes because she could always tell a ready mango: nothing, and she hurled the offending fruit toward the produce boy. Her sense of smell was really gone, and now there was also this disfigurement. *My disfigured self* in the cheeses and yogurts. In the open refrigeration, she was so cold, her nipples hardened until they fell off, then she felt other parts of her go, go missing, become a phantom limb, finger, liver, ear, her womb flopped out into the boxes of chilled pastry dough.

Of course what was happening was the body closing off its memory, for where does the self hold memory? In cheek, womb, sex, in kidneys deep in the back (or so the ancients said), in the olfactories—what better memory-sense than smell? And what better repository for the memory of the perfect puckered mouth of your son than the startled dark nipple? So this was protection from the pain of remembering, but she didn't understand that at the time. She only knew she was lessening in the world.

Though maybe she understood *something* in that dairy section when she saw a teen girl in a skimpy T-shirt with her arms folded across her chest, no bra, either hiding that her nipples were hard or holding her breasts on so they didn't fall off because of the overwhelming memory they held. But the girl didn't *want* to not remember: she was short of breath for the memory of a hot callused hand that cupped her; her eyes swam for his face in the unreal light while she was trying to choose for her mother, who was griping about her taking too long, the Blue Bonnet or Land O Lakes butter, salted or un, and the girl felt, too, her own mammary glands undisturbed and dormant and the trembling question in that dormancy, and Rizpah could see this girl sweetly aching out loud to hold on and relive the memory of the night before. And there was Rizpah: standing in a puddle of her own relinquished body parts because how could she ever bear to remember again? She narrowed, she contracted, she lessened, she blustered past the teen girl and the endless boxes of butter, dropped her basket that held no fruit and ran for the parking lot while she still had legs to run.

Maybe it was then that the other girl, the milky pubescent girl working checkout that night in her Kroger smock, saw that this would never work out, the grieving woman would never survive without help. She would no doubt go crazy, and worse. The girl trailed the woman to the Stagecoach, then to the river. She started shoplifting from the snack aisle after midnight.

Jessie van Eerden

Mistakes She Made As a Mother

She had favorites. She disliked the one with Saul's dark inky hair. Once, she locked herself in her bedroom and let her newborn cry for hours, milkless. Once, she lied to the middle son when he asked if he would ever die. She knew she heard the fence clinking the night they came for the boys and hooded them and never let them see the light again. It was as if someone had clinked open a music box, that delicate unlatching sound, so slight, when the lid rises and the ballerina unfolds into a ready pirouette, each time in a slow spin of sameness, and maybe she—Rizpah—did not want to unfold that night, was too tired to see who was at the yard gate clinking the chainlink.

And she made stupid mistakes: gave them Hershey bars for supper, kept forgetting to lock the cabinet with the Clorox in it, didn't teach the youngest to swim, shamed the third for crying (the third was too tender). She compared them, coddled them, spoiled them, struck them (but only twice and only because they'd played with fire). But the worst mistake, the deepest one abiding, lodged in her bones (as it turns out, the bone is a part of her body that cannot dismember), is the one that teeters her on the edge—she studies this mistake, for it's a wraith, so intangible and unreliable, she can't pinpoint it and confirm it, but she knows it. She wonders it aloud again and again: It's true that she asked, somewhere inside herself, to be alone, to have them gone—*Leave me alone*—didn't she say it brusquely when they asked her to fly kites with them, or to seek out the tree frogs that can never be found?

Reconsidering the Job

The natural question now is whether or not she wants to die. There would be a usefulness in it: it would relieve the birds that dodge her stones; it would allow the hyenas a feast of her body still warm, no longer fleshy, but with bone marrow still spongy; it would end the Kroger girl's commute and keep her out of trouble for shoplifting; it would get Rizpah out of this blinkered town where people pass on the bridge and hurl things, like crushed cans and insults and spare change and, worse, platitudes (*It gets easier with time*), and, worse yet, pieces of their to-go dinners. Sometimes they toss down the Classifieds from the Sunday paper which flutter to a flop on the rocks.

On one side of the page, the advice column: how to clean the shower drain with a coat hanger and baking soda. On the other side: Help Wanted. Secretarial again. Something useful.

So the real question is whether or not she wants to be useful. (*It would do you good*, some woman spits down between the bridge rails.)

But when would she have time? She is hard at work apprehending the blueness of the shadows and learning how to be alone (the milky girl and her contraband notwithstanding), and how to tremble. This is hard work, learning how to tremble, listening for what the bones are saying by trembling (she must tune into the bones since of course the other parts are not reliable: they disappear capriciously and take their secrets with them, just as they take their memories). Then there is this business with the beasts and birds, daily, nightly, scattering them back to the woods, which comes back to the question of dying, for if they suck her bones, the boys will be next.

She believes in her work—no, it's too much to say she believes in her work, that is going too far. But the way she goes at it…. It's like the young feverish artist, the amateur with paint in her hair and singularity of mind, foregoing sleep and food, mad for painting after painting, though there's only a goat-hair's difference between one to the next, the shade of red rustier, or the mouth just slightly downturned into a new kind of comma; she is trying to understand the secret of the face, trying to get the attention of the famed who will never look her way because she's in an attic freezing and painting with stolen or homemade paint in a buzzing city and there is no rent money but she cannot release the secret of the face.... It is like that. The answer to the question of whether or not Rizpah wants to die is like that.

The Rooms Inside

A teenage boy and his father ride by on a motorbike, father driving with son in back, the boy's arms crossed over his own hammered chest, not wanting to hold on—how close that would be, arms around the father's waist. Where to put his hands? At the belly button, the seat of life? Where the bloodfood pumped in? The boy's young arms want to ring a girl's waist and have been preparing—sinew and bone and muscle—for that arc, but, no, he won't buckle onto his father now, with his hands too near his father's sex. His sister could, his sister could cling as they banked the steep curves and as the fear of falling buzzed white in her head.

Rizpah doesn't throw the rock she's picked up, only watches, hears. *I've lost you,* she hears the father think as he speeds up, boots stupid on the boot rests because they can't sense at all through the soles. How have they come all this way, he and his son, and by which road? The greater speed because the greater shyness and longing, she understands the revving and raking engine. *Which life to live of all the ones inside me?* the father thinks to the son. *You were one of the ones inside me, now on the outside—I saw it the first time when you flew the kite, the string you held wrapped around a stick, we were two and I didn't know you. Just like that.* She nods, says, *Yes, I know,* and she wonders if her own noisy thoughts are interfering.

Rizpah drops her stone to the dust and thinks of the teen girl in the dairy aisle in Kroger—how many weeks, months ago?—how she folded her arms across her chest, but for a reason different from this boy's: she was aching loudly, but he aches silently, down deep and with great resistance; he carries the hurt in the small of his back because he sits like a rod, not touching, the curves so dangerous. It's like sleeping next to a body that doesn't touch yours—she remembers that with Saul, just for a flash—that is one of the rooms inside. How many rooms are inside a life? Hard to tell when the windows are all boarded up. Do *rooms* mean memories? Not exactly. Or maybe. Rooms are the several lives lived at once or subsequently or in spirals touching back on each other again. She realizes she can move through herself as through a house (there in the doorway: her mother, a silhouette) (in the cellar: her brother and buckflesh). She doesn't remember, she just moves, sees. She gets to the room where the third son is: the dangerous delicate light there too soft. As if it has just snowed over a skylight, but of course there is no snow here. She tries to sit in the corner of the room, which is only a crag in the rocks; she puts a flower in her horrible hair, hums absurdly.

In this room, squatting, she flutters her hands at the beasts and says *Don't feed on them* because she knows that the boys will wake up at any moment and want to go to school. That third one, pubescent, will want to shave for the first time, and he will lower his legs into the cloudy water pool so he can watch the legs of a girl lower too (a girl like this milky one that comes to see her—maybe that's why she comes, maybe she knew one of the boys, they wrote notes, kissed in the shed, but he's too tender, she would have hurt him probably, but even that sweet sting of a girl's scorn Rizpah would have loved for him to know)—their legs all concealed but not concealed by the wavy water, the wonderful tease rising between his own legs. How beautiful in the blue water, he laughs. This room is the opposite of memory since it is something that will never be. And the non-memory is fleeting. It won't be held onto, it comes as it chooses, like a teen boy, and the kiss bestowed on the mother is a whim of his; when he feels like acknowledging her, she has to settle for that, since he is moody most of the time, too sensitive (that third son), ratty T-shirt, baggy jeans, ballcap making his eyes glower (it's true he was her favorite), his hair like fine down, out of her reach, out from under her curtain except when he chooses. The craggy rock is damp upon her face pressing into it. She is at-the-mercy-of. The motorbike is still waspy with sound in the air, its motor so mean, but she can see the two of them no longer—*wrap around his waist, wrap around his waist...*

The Interview

Even so, she agrees to the interview. Trash blows down to the river all the time, and this morning the Classifieds rustled at her feet. Secretarial— she skimmed the ads. There was one for a paper bag company wanting someone self-sufficient, organized, flexible, personable, punctual. She whispered in one pigeon's ear, if it's ears they have in their dull heads (she doesn't know the anatomy of birds). Her hair is down to her waist now and looks like what a coat hanger would pull out of the shower drain she does not have. It's not self-respecting hair, but she has set up the interview anyway, with the pigeons cocking their heads, looking on, coming up with their questions. The pigeons have lice. Rizpah wades into the river to spruce up. Hartley & Sons Paper Products, Inc. She goes dripping into the front office with her freshly mudded hair, sits in the chair across from the desk. She says, *I'm here for the interview*, and divides her hair to sit evenly upon her shoulders. *You interview me for this job and I will answer from the stone in my mouth.*

Her Brother

Why is she thinking of her brother this morning? He was bookish, three years older. Forced to hunt with the others though he hated it and would shoot only when their father set his squared head near the son's neck, so close, and pointed out the deer's tentative approach to the stream, those footfalls (the closest he and their father ever came to touching). Only once did her brother hit his target, and with terribly perfect aim, so the death was quick and so too the gutting and the men's pats on his shoulder blades. Rizpah took her small hands and did what she could for him. She helped him wrap the meat in freezer paper and mark it, pound by pound, the tenderloin and roast: they traded in buckflesh and felt for the heartbeat that was not to be felt again. It was then that she started to listen to what people would say about God, things she heard the wind whistle: *God does not leave you comfortless.* She knew what they meant, but she stroked her cheek with the buckblood on her fingers and knew, crouching by her brother, that it was true God doesn't leave you comfortless only because God does not leave, God stays there without comfort too. You are comfortless, but God is there, jutting into the dirt with toes and fingers, making a little mud because of the drops of blood, and God has nothing to say, simply moves the stones around in the mouth wishing they were chewable and soft.

This time in the cellar with God, with her brother and his not-too-sturdy but sturdy-for-her back (because he shouldered her): this before the before the *before*; this was the pre-mother self, the pre-no-wife, no-widow, and she moves through herself as through a house, from the cellar room into the room where a sheer curtain flaps about with no effort (so differently than her beast-warning flag) and the curtain is not on fire and the two of them sing and realize they adore each other, not knowing that this kind of safe brother-sister love has a perimeter. They run from the room, giddy, and they hike to the narcissus plot and find them all blooming, of all the times to stumble into *narcissus*, the bloom-faces light yellow with fierce orange mouths. She tries so hard to smell the plot now, from her rock by the hanging dead, that unthinkable sweetness, but she can't, of course she can't.

A Dream of Kites

She stands on a hill not welcoming the wind. She knows what it will bring. She longs for solitude. This is unseasonable, it's winter with a warm spell whipped with wind which means a day for kites, and their boy-hands work at it all morning, to catch up with the wind before it dies, or goes elsewhere. They build the kites from dowels and newsprint, lace and coffee filters, screen mesh, T-shirt sleeves, ribbons. *Come fly,* they plead, and her voice is too sharp, *No, go on,* as her blown hair webs her face and hides her away, her dress wrung by the gusts and trapping her legs where she stands. The boys run ahead and she stays apart and it is almost sundown so the kites pink up in perfect light as they shrink into the sky. The trimmings tear off but the paper bodies stay solid and what she knew would happen happens, watching the youngest let out more string: *You were one of the ones inside me, now on the outside—I see it for the first time when you fly the kite, the string wrapped around a stick, we are two and I don't know you. Just like that. Strangers.*

The wind pastes her dress to her body, each of her curves tight unto linen so it's difficult to move, it is slow, but she makes it to the youngest whose head comes only to her navel, and she is not magnanimous, no: she grabs the spool of kite string from his hands and holds tightly, trying to rein it in, to bring the speck of translucent color back to the ground. It won't be called back, she grips the spool more and more tightly round, frantic, trying to memorize his small face at the same time.

And that's when she wakes on her rock by the river, and her hand is not on a wound spool at all, but around the neck of a bird, one of the smallest, one that has grown familiar with her. Dodging her stones and her swats, it often sleeps in her hair with its head tucked behind the lobe of her left ear as if about to tell her a secret, but it never speaks, and she has nearly killed it now—must have grabbed it in her sleep. She holds the tiny throat, feeling with her thumb the little bird heart like a white blister to burst, and she doesn't want to let go because the kite will be lost, the boy will cry. She holds tightly and, oh, she can feel the heart like a tiny seed, loose and unencumbered by a large and clunky chest bone like hers. Just a grape seed loose in pulp and pressed, and pressed. But the eye of fright and appeal gets through to her dream-mind and the kite colors fade. She cannot call them back. She cannot save them. She cannot save the self that refused them. She saves the only part of her that can be saved: the thumb at the bird's throat: lifting it, she lets go. Or, anyway, unpins the thing, but still softly rings the neck. Pets. Howls.

She Turns Down the Job

They've offered it to her. She chews some dried bananas left in the bag from the girl and sits there with her eyes fixed on the slightest bruise on one of the bodies, a rusted purple on his upper thigh that has not faded (they hang naked, these bodies). She convinces herself it is a bruise. She thinks how she has no job, no prospects. No pluck. Now they've offered her one, out of the blue, which is strange, considering the interview. The pigeons conferred and got back to her, are asking her to start Monday. But she turns it down—and why? Maybe because she wants her life back and knows she can't have it, so she has the sense of having no past and no future: without a future, you can't have a job. You can't start again. You can't wake up and visit the disastrous mirror and go into work. You can't agree with the advice slung at you, *Each day gets a little better* (someone has yelled that to her from the bridge).

The milky girl loves her for turning down the job. But the girl loves her for nothing, too.

You're going to love this, the girl says the next day. She has brought a wig for Rizpah, hot pink, from The Dollar Tree. All frizz and poof. And it's this, of all things, that makes Rizpah weep. She realizes that, impossibly, she has not yet wept and so she starts and does not stop for a long time. It is a long weeping, the kind that presses into her and out from her: it's the world trying to break in, needing to, and she needs to let it, and trying to break out from her rock-hard head, her head buzzing white with the fear of falling into something bottomless.

God also weeps over the offering of the dollar-store wig, or else God knows nothing about weeping.

A Discussion of Weeping

It is odd that she *didn't* weep, not for months, and when she finally *did* she could not isolate the cause of her weeping—even though the pink wig was the sure trigger—because the word *grief* was too small and the carnage of her boys too big and the heartbreak of the world like something way out in orbit, constellating with the empty places inside her. Back when she *didn't* weep she must have longed for it because weeping peals now from her vocal cords like thunder and permits all things, requires no thing beyond the weeping itself. And back when she *didn't*, there was that damned assault of joy—the tree frogs and the lilac chiffon dress, joy that streamed out behind her like yellow-white-blue streamers from bicycle handlebars in the roadwind. Back when there was that attack of joy, she was dry-eyed and accountable, she was criminal. She was the bad mother that did not cry for her boys.

There were of course the weeping cherry trees along the riverbank that she bent her stubborn bones to model after, to try to get the tears to come—old trees that sagged and dragged the ground with their long twigs. And when the man came to the river to prune them he said he had to do it in late summer or fall so sap wouldn't bleed from the cuts as bad, and she said, *Which is it then, late summer or fall?* because she had lost all sense of time, but he didn't answer.

The raven's voice, like a belly tearing open: the *not*-weeping can be like that. Like skin flayed, and, without skin, all the parts she's losing will seriously be lost forever and not simply misplaced for a time, lost somewhere inside the sack of skin.

There is the sadness of a good mother that everyone thinks she's supposed to feel—except for the milky girl with her pink wig and a floppy laugh and the Hostess Twinkies she's pocketed.

People who pass by have wrapped Rizpah's face in this sadness, a thick gauze, and it's been so hard to breathe. She gets so angry sometimes, goes livid, over the expectation of and demand for sadness of a very particular taste which she can't even taste because she cannot smell a thing. They all expect her to go crazy with grief, and this is why she throws rocks at the birds, even the swallows, the tanagers, the chickadees (she has learned a few more of their names) with their infinitesimal songs, for she has been gentle with her hands her whole life, as expected. She has done what is expected. But there remains no work to do for gentle hands. No job.

So when the weeping comes—triggered by the ridiculous wig stolen from the toy aisle of The Dollar Tree—it comes toward the end of the seven months of sitting on that smooth rock by the river (or toward the middle? What month is it? How many moons have peeked full? How many times has she bled the expected but unexpected blood?). It comes blue shadowed, black. Peal after peal, with no lightning, no rain, but she doesn't care whether it rains or not. It comes in its own time. And why must all this take so long?

Because that is how long it takes.

She goes back to the beginning, to the tale of kings and the tale of some God to be bargained with who is no God at all (*after all that, after the boys were offered up, after things were rectified and righted, God heeded supplications for the land, God granted the rain,* that is what everybody will say). God understands that the story never moves in a straight line, or else God understands nothing. The story swirls, spirals, loops, goes backwards and in between and tangles up. In between the words and the increments of time is where God is, if God is anywhere at all. God is in between the weeping and the not-weeping. God is in the curve of the stone.

Some will ask: What did she do on holidays? On their birthdays? (They would build kites on their birthdays until they had outgrown that.) Did she weep then because of course she would remember their play and their dancing at the feasts, dressed up like comic book heroes, and how the youngest, too excited, had slept in his hero outfit and crawled, warm like a cat, from bed to tell her something she could no longer remember? But to her the day is a vessel of darkness or of light, and she does not exercise preference even between these two things. The days are unremarkable.

The weeping has simply come when it has come, and it lasts long, who knows how many hours, days, weeks. The girl is there for most of it, but has to work a checkout shift in the middle somewhere. The weeping has no real beginning or end: it is a breaking-in and a breaking-out. And afterward, she lifts her less-hard head and thinks it must be morning because there is dew that feels different on her face than the tears did.

The Livid Body Is a Living Body

The morning after the weeping, her hair nested out behind her head with a few small birds still sleeping, Rizpah is cold and feels that if she could nestle into snow it could be warm. She notes the dried tomato seeds and the girl's leftover fried chicken that looks hurt, and all at once her body goes rigid. It goes gnarled, scaled over like an armadillo, and leaves no chinks open to the sadness that can enter even enamel things, like the teeth (that pain in her molars). Hand on her clunky chest bone, which she thinks is too large, she goes livid: a spike of light behind her eyes widens, her mouth opens like an infant's for the nipple, no sound— or maybe there is sound but her remaining senses simply sever ties and make a run for it: sound is over there by the river, vision over there among the pigeon-shit rocks, touch out of reach, smell nowhere, and no place taste.

Lividness is a kind of feral animal that carries the spike of light upon it, like a streak of bleached hair, and survives.

She has emptied out and now she goes livid on the rocks so sadness cannot invade the hardest of her bones.

Well, sadness is the least of it. There are the gossamer dangers to steel against—like gratitude, which tries to pry her open without warning, without source (deep wet flower pulled apart for the seeking tongue of some unnamable bird)—she would never recover. So she bulls around in a rage; she fumes and flails; she is brusque with the milky girl, not ever saying thanks for the Twinkies, for the jalapeño chips, for the electric pink wig. No, she would not recover from thanks whispered to the girl who now starts painting Rizpah's fingernails with great effort and care—she must yank Rizpah's hand down in the midst of the fit and fury (Revlon, Aisle 4, stolen). The girl leaves the dirt caked to the cuticles, black upon the quick, dabbing whenever Rizpah pauses, heaving, but Rizpah huffs off soon enough and stomps, then comes back to the smooth rock and drops her hand down, and the girl takes it again, applies the cheap red polish to another jagged nail.

Rizpah leaps, billows, takes off like a bullet.

With whom is she livid and why? With the girl? With the pigeons whose throats are target practice? With anything that moves or anything that doesn't, like the hanging deadweights, depending on the mood of the wind? She looks steaming at the dead—is she livid with the boy bodies, the strangers that they are (for how could she not be a stranger to the dead boy with the skin spread and popped apart at the puncture, how could she comprehend that body)? Is she raging at her brother and mother and people pulling back into themselves like beetles curling slowly away from fire until you look more closely and see they are *on* fire and curling to a curve of ash, consumed? Is she livid with the people up on the bridge who say *One day at a time,* when the easing-work of time only makes her become a stranger to herself? Is she livid with herself? For the stranger she is now? For the way, if she wrote the boys letters now, with enclosures—mementoes or feathers or sea glass or twig—she would have nothing to say, unable to conjure their faces sharply in her mind—their faces are unsharp—though she used to leave them letters under their pillows when she knew they were too shy to receive the words outright, like when the oldest fell in love and was spurned and his world crumbled (maybe she did that right)?

Is she not livid for the love so resilient in the burnt-beetle carcass, love's horrible persistence, like the growing of hair from the skull of the living and the dead, persistent despite all estrangement?

It would be more sensible to be incensed with David, the boy king, and the cowards taking orders to drive the stakes in between bones smelling—that once—of limes. Yes, of course—and with the bystanders who watched it, the sun that shone on it, the guardians of God that keep God's mute musty face out of sight, like tall men with tall hats in a crowd and she's too small, punching at the backs of their thick legs, their heavy suede coats like stage curtains she wants to set fire to. And livid with God and God's mumble mouth, and with the misplacement of her kidney, and with that damned fox that doesn't dare dart for the boys' blackened feet—*don't you dare*—and with Saul's touch when she was fifteen—*don't you dare*—but he dared and she had no say, arms bendable like the shamed clipped wings of fowl fattened for the butcher block. Oh and then, so livid with her *self* when she tried to love it and accepted the chiffon dresses and dresses and spread her body for him—*wrap around his waist, wrap around his waist*—because she wanted so badly to capture something she could keep, as though with a sieve, but it all poured through, too fast and too fine, along with all she had been before she was collected for the king's chambers. Before the before the before— at the height of her rage she sees herself as the girl trading in buckflesh, taking the corners too fast, running, and her body a force—the girl who collected agate rocks and did not throw them but put them in a pouch then ran home alone, outran them all and slipped off, no one knew where to, coming into the kitchen just barely and her mother stirring a pot not knowing the panting girl was there, girlbody unseen, unheard, undiscovered, uncollected, only her panting breath from running so fast. It was that kind of alone then, exhausted and full. And now, panting after her rage, her lividness, it is a different kind of alone. Yes: to be left is different than to be not yet found.

No, she is not angry with the milky girl. But the girl bears the brunt.

Rizpah has stormed and kicked and thrown. She is worn out, worn to a nub and a heap, with seven of ten fingernails painted red.

Magnificent, says the girl.

I need no magnificence. I never did.

I know.

Sometimes I am angry that I cannot kiss them. You cannot kiss the face when you cannot smell the skin.

The girl nods, recaps the Revlon bottle.

Rizpah lives.

From somewhere, somehow, the girl brings over a hot towel coiled into the shape of a rose, deep and wet in its folds, like something from first class on a transoceanic flight—where did she get such a thing? It is warmth on the face.

I cannot thank you, Rizpah whispers.

I know.

It's too dangerous.

I know.

Even rigid, taut, Rizpah's skin sighs, her very skin.

Things She Did Not Expect

That sanity would feel so cold after the volatile weeping and raging, and would arrest her like a sudden storm front seizing the night air. That she would wake sane and calm, shoo a silver fox from a boy's black waterless toe, then work on a stick fire, humming. That she would establish a routine and that, though the bottom would drop out and though the fear of falling would buzz white in her head, she would somehow not fall forever. She did not expect to shiver in the arms of sanity—she should have gone crazy, by all rights, into hot flame. This all ought to have done her in. She did not expect that sanity could hold her like a depression in the deep snow she has dreamt about, like an empty high-sided metal bowl.

One Day She Decides to Decorate

The pigeons say she's severe. Harsh, they say. But what do they know? They're stubborn, ungainly birds full of themselves. They stand apart and stare and gurgle. The younger, tinier birds—sometimes as tiny as a single dyed feather in a carnival headdress—are not full of themselves but nervous in the night. Where she lies on the rock they nestle into her hair for comfort. But if she is to be comfortless so will they. She pokes at their bellies and at their tweezer-tip beaks tucked under their wings—why? What is she asking of them? They cry out in a shrill confetti of chirps that turns her outspread hair into a tree canopy for one full minute of complaint, which is what she was asking for, demanding, like any insomniac: others' wakefulness when she is awake.

In the morning, the pigeons huddle, disapproving. The sleepless little birds stagger, dazed, into flight as if into a sky of molasses. She wonders if maybe they're right—the pigeons—maybe she is too severe. She looks around and has a singular magnanimous moment: she decides to decorate for them. She surveys and scouts; the sunrise disappoints her, its colors all blurred today, and she wants distinctness between things. She wants a block of sky discolored, like just before a tornado, then another block clear blue and almost transparent through to the subtle stars, then a section of pink that is the clean fingernail down to the quick, the feeling-life. She will build this sky on her rock for them, with leftover wrappers, magazine inserts that have blustered down to the river rocks, tabloid pages the milky girl swipes, a neon shoe lace that is very near the color of quick. She scatters a few strands of the pink wig that's frazzling, and so she makes sky on the ground. A sky so near the bodies of the dead that she suddenly thinks the ground-sky is a kind of heaven for them. And why not? Call it Sheol, call it Hades, Hell, the Outer Dark, but there are frizzy strands of pink to spruce it up. She puts on the frayed, picked-over wig, a catastrophic halo of electric, and the little birds do laugh a little (if they can be said to laugh). The pigeon jury finds other things to do, and she starts on a neighboring slate rock, papering it with a cut-up carton; she moons around, unhinged and muttering, gathers something she'll call linoleum. *Go on* (to the pigeons sitting high) *tend to the world with your discerning stare, there is no saving me.* Mooning, humming as the day takes stock of her work and she takes stock back, upon her papered sky. *I need no saving.*

Jessie van Eerden

Day of the Fly

It is morning again. She studies the huge green metallic eye of the deer fly. It's dreadfully wide unto the world, and bulbous. Refracted inside are the hyena, the blistered birch bark, the sack of dried currants left behind by the weeping cherry pruner. Of course the boys are refracted there too, and their naked yellowpus bodies acquiesce to the eye's curve so that they're changed into bendy acrobats.

But inside the green itself is where she goes, peering deeply, rocks hanging still and heavy in her hands at her sides. Sometimes she can hit even a deer fly, a wasp, a cricket dead-on, and she was about to. The fly's wings are also unmoving—both of them, she and the fly, are suspended in a kind of amber, no wind or unrolling of time for a moment. She is thirsty for green, though it's dangerous. Before she knows what she's doing, she clambers inside the green, studying its walls and tunnels with her arms and legs and fingertips, like a soft-footed spider, recalling, once inside the green metal, that phosphorescent joy of the tree frogs spurting from their secret tiny mouths, and then the bright green beneath that (since there is always a beneath): lush moss, her first sex with the boy who hid a rough onyx for her in his pocket under layers and layers of robe that he removed, and he gave her the onyx for a bracelet. She held it to her lips then undid her dress—his eyes, too, so green—and they were fourteen and her whole body shivered on the shore of a very different river that was bedded with moss and not stone upon stone upon stone.

She had raced home after—wholly uncaptured—and found her mother scraping a new animal hide in the doorway, and when her mother looked up at her, she—the young Rizpah with black smooth hair let down to her waist—felt no shame, and her mother issued forth no shame, and the daughter said, without having to speak about the wet of the green moss and how deep he came inside her, *I have had some real happiness.*

And the mother said, *Yes, and that is why you are sad for the first time.*

And the daughter felt that it was true: a sadness rimmed her happiness and let off a faint fog of light. She hadn't seen it before, as she'd run home trampling the duff of the forest floor, hadn't seen it in her hair or under her nails, but she saw now that the sadness was there.

Her mother, deer hide dangling from her hand like a child she almost didn't want, rose in the doorway—always in the doorway—and could see the palm reader was right, could see the sadness that would ravage her daughter in the years to come when the king would bend back her arms and the boys would burst out of her body, one by one, and then out of the world, all at once; could see her girl's weedy hair and table-rock bed and her lying-down and rising-up in beast-beating vigil, and the mother knew that this trembling first love and the rich black heart of the beautiful onyx Rizpah held meant the beginning of her daughter's meshing with the world. This was the beginning of the grieving and the loss of scent, and, *still*, the mother said *Yes* she would help string the onyx for the bracelet because she knew, despite everything, the green thing deep in the girl's center was—impossibly—worth it all.

Inside the metal bulb of the deer fly eye, Rizpah backs up, scoots forward, backtracks again, edgy then patient then still, as if stunned: she sees her mother in the doorway, hide in hand, laughing and unstringing her own pearls to give wire for the bracelet, and she knows now what her mother knew then. Inside the green metal of the eye, *my God*, today she finds something inside herself that does not taste like kitchen sponges. The surprise—it hurts, *my God, my God...*

The Rooms Inside

And sometimes the many rooms inside only remind her she is empty, a solitary duchess saddled with an estate. It's the price of expansiveness: the still and stale air that remains after the expanding, air that's held, waiting to then be filled with moving bodies and talk. But there is no one, except, now and then, her earlier selves: girl weighted with the onyx bracelet, girl doing a math problem, girl brushing her hair after a first swim when legs had felt more like fins. Girl who had such beautiful thoughts once, who ran fast, who loved her brother, who wondered what it would be like to have a child. And these girls have such blindnesses that sometimes she can't bear them; they ignore her anyway.

So she goes through and turns on all the lights so that, from any angle from the road or tree line or bend in the river, the window glow will invite the stranger in, but she doesn't know whether he will come in or not. She raises the windows, too, and lets in the night sounds— tree frogs, some sputtering of leaves—hoping she might hear him pass, whistling or something. Nothing stirs but the smaller troublesome sounds, and the big house feels so empty, the sheer curtains cheap, no longer evoking a day when her soul flew. She brews some coffee, sets elbows on the table. God is the stranger she wants to welcome or God is nobody at all, but people think if you welcome the stranger the stranger will simply stop by—just like that—because you are magnanimous, and, anyway, she knows she is not magnanimous and her mind grows dark because no one comes. She passes the night alone, listening to the stifling spaciousness in all those many rooms she thought were beginning to free her, rooms that *have*, in fact, begun to free her as she spreads out, contracts less, but there is something beneath freedom, then something beneath that. Always a *beneath*.

And where there is some expansiveness, there is also emptiness within the wide, blurred outline, but neither one negates the other: they simply can't exist apart. Knowing this or not, Rizpah feels herself longing, oddly, for the Stagecoach Motel, its cool tiles above the constricted ring of steamy tubwater, the grouting she traced, the impulse to duck under and stay there and stay there. She misses the restriction of the stale room and longs for narrowness to return, for a going-backwards. This longing is more dangerous than gratitude's peeling of the rough skin down to the tender skin, because this weary longing is the longing to die. (The milky girl standing at her cash register catches the scent of danger like a hound and knows she must act fast; she sloughs her Kroger smock, starts running for the airy house by the river by the boys by the trees along the tree line rippling with ready hyenas.)

From the kitchen table, Rizpah sees a slip of a person get created by the porch light—Oh, Rizpah thinks, just the pesky girl with some Kroger-brand sodas. The girl darts in the screen door and soundlessly pulls Rizpah back from the perilous ledge she didn't know she was standing on (was it not simply a kitchen table?). With snack crackers and fake cheese, Rizpah is plied, more or less. And, in foil, a cold baked potato that she didn't want the first time around, and she turns her face from it now, again, but she does nibble a cracker. She doesn't notice the sweat and panic of the girl, the mud up to her knees because she raced there through the marsh and the heather, how the girl's heart now calms a little, not so frantic though not at ease—Rizpah doesn't even know the girl has saved her. Rizpah is sure she does not need saving. She is sure there is no saving her.

And, at Last: Who Is the Milky Girl?

This girl who comes to her?

What are these?

Dried mango, the girl says.

Rizpah sniffs, sniffs more deeply: nothing. Refuses the leathered strips.

The girl has an inconsistent gait, sometimes a light little soft-shoe and other times heavy and dragged through the droughted riverbank dust as she whispers things like, *I'm glad there's at least a river in Hell.* It's her skin Rizpah notices, so bright and clear and untouched—but maybe it is touched, Rizpah thinks one day, or *has been* touched, watching the girl watch the third boy's bones move in her wake and rattle like wind chimes as she passes by. The way the girl watches the third one, with a claim—did they—? Had the two of them—?

I don't need saving.

True, but you need looking after.

I don't need looking after, Rizpah says, grabs the Styrofoam cup of coffee the girl has brought.

There are dresses I haven't worn in months, Rizpah says, setting down the coffee to unknot a dead bat from her weedy hair. *There's a lilac one.*

What's the lilac one like?

Like all the buttons are in the perfect place. Up the chest, down to my bellybutton.

Chiffon? The girl finally turns from the boy-bone wind chime.

Yes. Chiffon. Rizpah lays down the bat with its wings wrapping itself in a doomed cocoon. *I want my dresses.*

I know where they are, and you can't go there.

Bring me my dresses.

The girl is not sure, but *Okay*, she says, and goes to the Stagecoach and gets the key from the front desk and finds dresses and dresses still hanging in the closet of the narrow room. She hurries.

An armful of chiffon and taffeta and silks, simple cottons too, lazy housedresses but even those have fitted waists, so perfect.

A fox comes scavenging and Rizpah runs at it with the flag and it whimpers away, then nothing. No stirring. So the two of them turn to the heap of dresses which all hold the awful memory of the body that wore them once—and where has that body gone? Rizpah puts her hands to her body—no, it is not the same one. The two of them don't know what to do but stand there and let their eyes get used to the colors. Then:

The milky girl—who *is* she, this girl?—holds up the lilac one, shakes it out, pulls it down over Rizpah's awful head. And it starts. Rizpah pulls on all of them, one right after another, the buttons not straining, she has grown so thin. Each dress is a strange little rip in time, a flurry of red and plum and deep green with soft blue belts, until she has worn them all and peeled them all off her unwashed flesh and then finds again her pool of black vigil dress, a kind of kimono, eaten by moths and by the night, and she pulls it on, not angry at its tatters. She tosses up the bounty of dresses and they drift to the ground and the milky girl soft-shoes to one side of a wide rock then to the other side, laughing.

Is she someone inside Rizpah's self, this girl? Someone outside herself? Both? Does she go light? *Is* she light itself, or does she merge with light but not insist on it? Is she the one who comes running with a firecracker-heart—even if she explodes inside herself—to be with those who lie down next to death to make sure they do not die?

Is she the cashier at Kroger, a shoplifter, not so good at math? How is it that she has come to be someone kicking at the fluffed heap of dresses on the ground, urging Rizpah to try them all on again? *First the lilac one...*

In the Doorway, Her Mother: A Silhouette

Rizpah as a child: She wakes up, still warm from bed, little cat that she is, and hits the cold—the wood floor, the icy hammer of air coming down from the drafty windows fog-veiled. She pulls on jeans and a sweater quickly and, just as quickly, her mother gathers her up in the morning dark. Her mother slips out of the house, carrying her bundle of Rizpah, for a secret visit she would be ridiculed for if anyone knew.

In the palm reader's beaded tent, the old hand takes Rizpah's little cat paw, warm yet.

She will live long? her mother asks.

Yes.

She will have lovers?

Yes.

She will marry?

Silence.

She will marry?

She will bear children?

She will not be alone?

Rizpah blinks, once, twice.

Smuggling her little cat back home, the mother panics, rocks, scans the room into which dawn is creeping slowly with unstoppable increments of time. Rizpah blinks sleepy eyes, happy that the warmth she woke in has not altogether faded next to her mother's breasts and belly and coat and hair.

What is there to fear? her mother asks her.

Silence.

What is there to fear?

Nothing? Rizpah says.

Nothing, that's right, and every day she will ask her daughter this.

Here. Her mother stands and heads for the table vase of snowy Queen Anne's Lace. *Today I have an idea.*

Rizpah now, beside the river in Hell: There are times she holds the rock in her hand, intended for a starling, but then she is about to whale on herself instead, to go for the temple, to end it, like when she wanted to go under in the Stagecoach tub, that mausoleum of pretty tiles steaming, neat grout in a pattern she traced. Until she heard the helpless alley cats, but here there are no alley cats, so what's to stop her?

She wakes to a horrible guilt some days, with no one to care for and no mouths to feed, no longer a mother. One day she forces herself to—what?—stroke the milky girl's dull face to awkwardly suggest *daughter*—but the girl knows better, pulls away, disliking being fawned over. The girl knows it's a penance that Rizpah does not owe, knows so much more than her youth would seem to permit (and it is permission: the girl has given herself permission to know these things).

The girl jerks her face away like a jumpy horse and puts a fistful of Queen Anne's Lace in Rizpah's filthy hand.

For what? Rizpah asks.

For when it gets bad. And the girl takes off, pulling on her Kroger smock, late for her shift, perhaps nobody's daughter.

For when it gets bad, Rizpah repeats, with the stone in one hand aiming for her temple and with weed-flowers in the other. *When it gets bad, the foxes circle me like I'm Jericho.*

She crushes the Queen Anne's Lace stems together, the white heads dusting her gross skirt with a shower of tiny white blooms. She can't smell them, only stares at them. *Well, it's bad,* she says. Then: in the doorway, her mother: a silhouette. It's as simple as that this time, even if not every time—she sees a glimpse of her mother and so she does not want to die.

Mother—do you know what's become of me?

Rizpah as a child, a little cat kneeling in her brother's old jeans, watches her mother who has the big beautiful idea. Her mother pulls the weed-flowers from the clay vase and lays them out, retrieves four jars and fills them with water, and, in each, drips the food coloring: blue, green, red, yellow.

Come, she says, and Rizpah's small hands help trim the stems and arrange the snowy Queen Anne's Lace, which they'd picked from the roadside the day before, in each jar of colored water. *Just wait and see,* says her mother.

It is fall, it is Sunday, no school, they do chores together, distract themselves, but every few hours they come back around to observe the Queen Anne's white turning ever so slightly, light blue and a pink, drinking up the color. The plant veins, stout cell wall next to stout cell wall, firm yet supple with no self-restraint—they suck up the color with such thirst and, soon enough, the color spreads. Rizpah sleeps and wakes and the transformation is complete.

What a good idea, Rizpah whispers as her mother arranges the single bouquet in the clay vase again, ties bright yarn around the lip and gives it to her Rizpah. It is Monday, a school day, a cold day, but Rizpah is bundled for the school bus: she is taking the changed bouquet to enter into the flower contest at the festival. *What is there to fear? Nothing,* they repeat the daily refrain, and Rizpah's tiny self runs for the bus, careful with the vase. She boards and looks back out the window to the house: her mother is silhouetted at the door. Rizpah watches from the school bus window and in her lap: a bundle of Queen Anne's Lace blooming into a pale rainbow. The festival is that day, after school, and she'll enter the contest with the others for the best bouquet and she's nervous, but perhaps she will win the ribbon, because it was her mother's idea, and it was a beautiful idea, and she loves this fall festival, the exhibits, the flower arrangements and crafts and other contests, like vegetables made into little people, balloons made into animals—everything transformed—and the rides: Squirrel Cages, Tilt O'Whirl, the Zipper that hurls everyone in a squeezed yellow car that takes her breath.

Rizpah now, nothing but a rough vigil dress on a goat-hair rug on a rock by the dead, thinks, It's as simple as that sometimes. You enter the room inside where you see your mother in the doorway, in silhouette, and you see her big ideas—and so you don't wish so badly to die. In the doorway: black sweater, barn boots, and a silhouette that strangely glows in the dark (in time, the glowing silhouette quietly explodes: it does not explode, does not, does not, then—at the right time—it does, and the force of it is great). There is the oat straw that stuck to her black barn sweater, the foreknowledge of the fear that would assail her tiny girl-woman in the night with the circling fox and the sickly bear and the scroungers and scavengers vying for the bones of the months-long-dead. There is the girl-woman with kitchen sponges in the mouth, calling out from the sealed bus window as the bus carries her away, the bouquet in her lap: the good idea.

And of course her mother's biggest and best idea was the one disguised inside the bouquet, the one Rizpah would understand much later. The best idea would be to lie down next to death and not die. *Go on, go on. Go out into the world with your dyed batch of blooms and win a ribbon in the fall air and let yourself move through the rides and games with loose fingers: you must be ready to lose everything.*

Except the life inside your life.

This is the idea the mother pulled around her little cat Rizpah like the straw-stuck sweater around her shoulders, but not just to keep out the cold or to bring comfort, no, not like that.

Jessie van Eerden

Rizpah drops the rock to the dust. The blooms from the milky girl are pitiful and white. She buries her face in them.

Her Body Re-members, Though She Does Not Ask It To

Another morning, startling, like a slap. Lying on her back, and then she feels it. The hardness of her nipples, which means she feels her nipples at all—she hasn't since the dairy aisle episode in Kroger, when she saw the spectacular teen girl with her arms tight across her chest and across her longing, and she—Rizpah—lost one nipple then another among the fancier cheeses and ran. Tiny throbs now take her breath: they are alert and recalling stroke and suck and milk and heat. Like dark rose pecans. And it's slow as she lies there, and inexplicable, but she re-grows a limb, then finger, liver, ear. She feels the presence of things that you feel only after their absence—the part of her leg that the third one clung to when shy (the one who was too soft), the ring of ankle skin—burning a little as the skin cells fuse—growing back to remember an anklet of reeds.

It's just that I—

It's just that—

Now she twists a little, hands to her belly: a subtle wrenching there. She gets up and squats upon the rocks and doubles over, though not from pain exactly, and whips left and right and doubles over again—someone might think she were dancing. It's a globe, stretched, when it first grows back: like a lantern lit, her womb, like an oversize gooseberry, it tremors a little and rests down into its own ridged muscles that yield the memory of bearing a child, and the possibility of bearing again. *It's just that I can't*—yet she does, she can, hold the memory and the searing possibility. Her new innards are light-infused, squeezed and twisted into place and so bright, the unearthly color of a glow stick, all transfigured as if ready for something, for what transfiguration does, if you survive it, is put you in the way of danger again (meaning the gossamer dangers: gratitude, joy, love).

But what made this the day? The day when she can now bear the presence of a breathing womb and an earlobe traced by a tiny finger once? Who knows. Who decides these things. She smirks, she sits and stares out at the river, knees up and apart, the cold air rushing in between her legs to cool her.

And When Her Sense of Smell Returns—

Once the bowl of her stomach grew back with no cracks, and her tongue twitched to life, wet and inquisitive of her teeth, she began to feel suspense.

A goldfinch is caught in her hair this morning and she waits with uncharacteristic patience until it frees its yellow self, then she rises. *It's just that I miss hunger.* That's how it starts, and how to find hunger again? First find smell, then taste, then the hunger for the taste and then the seeking out of taste and the subsequent sustenance.

She finds an old bread crust and crumbles it into her palm. The finch comes back and pecks, dot by dot, quickly, since this capricious woman has targeted the finch with rocks plenty of times. Flurry of gold and it's gone, belly full.

She says to the disappeared bird, *God is hungry or God is nothing and nobody.*

It takes all day, though she can't will it to happen. She simply waits, in suspense.

It takes until the middle of that night and the first thing she smells is night itself, but even though she's spread-eagle on the goat-hair rug on the smooth rock by the river, she smells not *this* night but the night of her childhood home and so she returns to smell, at first, as her young self, the one that learned to drive on those curvy roads, with a brother who was shy of the gun and the killing but who traded in buckflesh in the cellar of cool stone, so cool you could keep milk down there, and they did: one door opens another.... It is the smell of lilacs, a bush she can't see and doesn't have to because lilacs can be smelled from miles away, along with the fetid nesting smell, of shit and old egg, of sparrows in the lilac branches. A gentle commingling, both scents at once, sweet and foul, not assailing her, but coming calm and slow into her nostrils. The lilac night, the secret wet night that netted her when she slept as a girl and kept off mosquitoes and dark dreams, then the summer-grass night munched by deer alert and joyful— that word again, *joy*—then the morning dark that follows and her mother at the screen door laced with that wraith-smell of coffee and cinnamon.

It's almost painful at first, a slight burning like she felt at her ankle: she can smell the boys' gone-ness. Not the yellowpus decay, she is spared that, it is over and the bodies are more harmless now in scent: they only smell gone. And there is that persistent lilac following from girlhood into now, subtle then forceful, as if to insist that it's not enough because it's not. She then smells the deep hues of the fruit before she sees it, there in a rock sink clear of pigeon shit. She picks up the nectarine with both hands and her cracked lips touch the flesh. She hungers for it and bites into it, and the taste is active, alive, it delivers her, carries her on its pain-shooting feet into hunger. She is hungry, and she eats.

But the milky girl hasn't been here for days.

Who has left this nectarine here?

The Impossible Scene

This is the scene promised by the tale: David, the murderous young king, ambles down to the river, scuffing over rocks, embarrassed and sullen like an adolescent. He comes to marry her. He comes with a velvet sack and she looks at his jeans and black eyes and tight shirt and she stands, folding her goat-hair rug in half then half again, like a tablecloth. Moody, without speaking, he helps her take down the bodies, as if taking in the wash, and he will finally bury the bones though they are no longer bones. No, they crumble into talcum stuff in their hands, so the two people are dusted by the dead. He tries to catch them all in the sack, but small poofs and clouds slip to the wind—maybe a hand, or a jawbone, a sex, a pair of lips, *poof*. But she lets them go and when he says, *Where should we bury them*, she shrugs. She is long past seeking out their burial: laser eyes, seeking sharply something other.

Have you heard God? he asks, posturing himself like a pigeon.
You haven't.
What have these months been like?
I was silent for awhile, then I wasn't. I interviewed for a job. Turned it down. I lost my sense of smell, and my kidney, and I think my liver and my womb. I studied their dangling feet, each whorl on the toe until the toe shriveled like a date. I studied them, like topographical maps, until the land folded in on itself and lost distinctness. Rizpah picks up a knife, one that the milky girl brought once for stick-sharpening.

David fidgets.

None of my thoughts were beautiful, she says.

When my liver grew back, she says, *it was like someone slipped a plum into my side, secretly. It felt like a plum.*

You've heard God then? Face almost petulant, but, beneath his petulance, such fear.

The stones in the mouth make it hard for God to speak. The knife blade smoothes back and forth over her vigil dress. *Maybe there are some things God doesn't know how to say. Does God have shadows inside, things hidden even from God? God's own light is cloudy.*

I swear I will never do it again.
You're just a boy.

Were you angry?
Livid.

Were you afraid?
Of what?

Did you go crazy?
Sometimes.

I'll save you, he says.
I don't need saving.
I'll buy you dresses, he says.
I don't need dresses.
What do you need?
Maybe I asked to be alone, closed up in myself. Careful what you ask for.
Maybe a bed?
What's a bed? The knife is still. So much talking. *My mother used to hold my jeans up to the fire to warm them before I stuck my legs in them. Sometimes that kept me alive down here, thinking of that.*
How?
Just the fact of it. Did you leave that nectarine for me?

What nectarine?

Later, some would call it a marriage, but it would be a tutelage, a training—this is how you lie down with the dead and do not die. He wouldn't need to know this to be king—you need to know nothing of significance to be king.

With those transfigured outlines of her face, it's clear she became someone new, not operating under the same linear storyline, like, simply: *You'll marry your sons' murderer.* She is mother and not-mother, he is murderer and child-shepherd, daydreaming, he is a fool. There are no psalms left in him; he wrote them all when he was a pensive kid shepherd, though, later, he'll be credited with a few that she'll write: *my heart is like wax, it has melted within me, my strength is dried up like potsherd, my tongue clings to my jaws, you have brought me to the dust of death.*

Dogs have surrounded me. I can count all my bones.

What complicates forgiveness is its impossibility.

What complicates impossibility is the mysterious appearance of a nectarine.

You smell, he says.

She says, *Smell me. You go on and smell me.*

A king's widow can only marry another king.

Fine. I'm no widow. No wife, no mother.

It smells like wet chicken skin, he says.

They talk about the chicken smell, they sit on rocks, he touches her awful hair, she says, *Don't,* and he stops. He says it's like chicken skin cold from an ice water bucket after the butcher and the scald. Yes, the feathers unstabbed from the bendable clipped wings, a rough progression backwards from birth when the feathers first speared through and fluffed out, first sleek, then soft—and then to end up nude again. They both—Rizpah, David—have butchered and so they know how the smell gets into your own skin when you carry them by their scaly feet. You smell like it for days, like a shamed chicken carcass headed for the soup pot. It smells you up for days.

Give me a piece of fruit, she says.

Why?

Because I smell fruit too, mingling with the stink of death. I smell everything now, and I can taste.

But you smell like rot.

That's the smell of God on me. Give me fruit.

And he did, a dinged-up peach, and her teeth sank in.

What do you mean the smell of God?

She lets the juice trickle down her chin. She's still retraining herself how to chew, how to savor. They sit like that for a long time. He asks questions in a sweat, trying not to watch the knife blade that's in her other hand, trying not to retch from the smell, or from the possible answers to his questions, and she answers only when she wants to. She puts her peach-juicy hand on her breastbone, disbelieving the heartbeat beneath, trying to out-turn her heart and wear it on her outsides, the big bloody thing, to give the air access to it, maybe turning it blue or black. People need to see the hard work of the heart.

People need to see the hard work of the heart, she says out loud. *But they won't. They'll see the tale of kings, the notations for the devout, the lessons on the frontlets—that's what will get passed down.* The juice on her hand turns the dirt there black.

They do write about you. Important people. About what you've done here before God.

And what is it I've done? They write about themselves, not me, not God.

He fidgets, droops his arms between his knees, all lost. He knows they'll marry, he'll get his way, but it won't matter. He says, *What will you do if I fall in love with you?*

She takes the knife, finally, to her hair, near the scalp, cutting free the living and dying bodies of small things that have nested and tangled themselves there. He is relieved that she does not stab him, his expectation of vengeance so predictable. He will always be a boy king trailing after the unsurprising imagination of kings. Surprise is what she aches for.

I want to be surprised, she says.

Someone keeps giving your life back to you, like a cold potato you didn't want the first time, the second time, and now must eat. *What do you love?* he asks, watching the silent rowers row past under the bridge's shadow.

She thinks over the seven months, or years, or centuries, whatever.

The dew, she says.

The dew?

There is something about the dew. How helpless it is. She lay on her rug on the rock by the river and the morning dark would unthicken to wisps of light and her face, as she woke, would be wet with dew until the sun made itself substantial and came to dry her. So it is fleeting—dew—it is indiscriminate and pointless as it coats and kisses and pearls upon the shriveled-date toes, upon the hair slipping from the roots of the scalps, moist, damp—there and then not there—only a suggestion and she would rise to it, and it would be gone. Only now is she aware that she loved this.

Jessie van Eerden

The Rooms Inside

At last, the disappointment can settle its restless self, like a tune rumbled around in a deep marbly voice, over time, a murmur sinking in: she will finally be a bride after years as a concubine. The texture of disappointment is pasty, and what does Continuing On mean or matter? Others' togetherness, when she climbs squinty-eyed out of the river crevice, after so many months, years, whatever, to see others milling, shopping, driving in cars together—she doesn't want it, their togetherness, not in this way. There is an aloneness now: she carries it, like a dense bulb in her belly. What does it mean to want? It exhausts her to think she'll have to learn the meaning again. Sounds are tinny and echoing, far away, in her ears, all the other voices; not the same as the gauze between her and everyone at the height of the pain, no, and not the kitchen sponges in her own mouth and ears. No, this is something other. Maybe there is nothing she wants, nothing she needs. Why the disappointment? It must be the disappointment of the bridal white, its isolation. Now it's hers too, the bride's loneliness. She has it after all, with all the others. (The palm reader knew...)

She's had to give herself permission to be alone (the milky girl and her contraband notwithstanding). And to lie down next to death and not die.

Finally a bride after her concubinage—did her mother foresee this? Yes, of course she did, the palm reader spoke and was also silent. The lonely-making dress, the untouchable dress—a bride for the first time, after losing everything. The white is laughable and won't do all, so she sends for the milky girl to find the lilac chiffon, but the girl is nowhere, vanished into her own life. She has slinked away, back to the cash register, but not only to the cash register, also to a young man she met in Aisle 4, and then into an opening of her own rooms, through a creaking door, a new door with new hinges, fresh paint, a springy bed, flowers in a jar for her, yes, that is how it should be. No one else is really around but David, his bangs in his eyes, his hangdog face. She sighs. The dress will turn up. In the meantime:

Let me tell you about rooms, she says, and he perks up, fidgets less when she talks.

She tells him more about her mother, of the doorway and of her mother's one big idea, and how the silhouette formed against the light in the room behind.

You have to go inside, Rizpah says to him. Her vigil dress looks like skin in places and her skin looks like her vigil dress, poor, glossy, crude. She is roughly bald now, by her own hand with the knife, and the air is cool on her head. His eyes fix on her.

She says again, *Let me tell you about rooms,* and she tells him about the tiny motel room at the Stagecoach with pretty tiles around the bathtub and the sharp Midwestern wind cutting up the dust and shivering down a constant layer of it onto the sill so that the sandy dust was in the air, in her hair, on her tongue. She says she decided not to die in that room so now it is in her, this room. The capacity inside is unlimited: once you realize you are nothing, you can harbor the world and all its harm and shame and joy—such volume.

How can the rooms just keep going? he asks.

Deeper and deeper like a network of underground caves that goes beneath and beneath even the floor of the sea. *There is always a beneath,* she says.

And how can they not be boarded up? That's what we do as we get older, we board up the rooms, the cellar, the room with the sheer curtain that trembled with happiness. There's the room she gave birth in, that room she's never yet visited, but she knows it's there waiting: its windows open to the sounds of a train, running feet, a mourning dove or two, and her own bed a frothed ocean.

You have come down to the river, she says, *how young, how murderous, speaker for God who knows nothing of God despite your hundred psalms people sing like pop songs on the radio. They're catchy.*

She rises, smelling his late adolescent odor, his nervousness. She takes this boy king's hand. Forehead to David's smooth forehead. *Your inside-rooms are yet unopened.*

They skip rocks together, waiting for the lilac dress to turn up. She has no intention of being a good wife. They weave reeds. It isn't love, it's something else, or maybe love is something else, and forgiveness is something else too, something no one knows, here in this circle of rocks with two people smelling like wet chicken skin (it has rubbed off on him too).

She lets David bury their bones, the fine flour crushed, dust in a velvet sack. And she agrees to marry him, as a member of the droughted world. But her laser eyes will continue to seek out the faces of those who grieve—there is always someone—those who have had to agree to the terms of the blue shadows. She will seek them sharply.

> *It will finally rain now,* he says.
> *It was never rain I wanted.*

It Was Never Rain She Wanted

In the end, what surprise is there in rain? Its pounding and soaking, its saturation. It drenches. It comes on its own terms, when it wants to, and can withhold for years so that the parched barley stalks bend in shame and shamelessly call it down, making a mockery of themselves. God does not withhold or send the rain. Rizpah considers this on the day of the wedding, perched as she is on her rock, birdlike, her fingertips trying to lengthen into wings with a broad wingspan. She is aware that all of her cocksure claims about God are no more binding than a king's. She senses that God is beneath God—like a seed in a covered furrow—or God is no place.

But she doesn't really know.

And, if not rain, then what is it she has wanted?

Isn't rain what everyone wants? The obvious thing? The way everyone wants a miracle? Like the people who passed above her, on the bridge, and gathered their coat collars to the neck, as though passing through a cold eerie mist, or tugged their pilled sweaters more tightly around them though the threadbare wool could not protect them from that specter scooting across her rock toward the dead, toward the fox's gleaming teeth. They thought she sat there longing for the macabre dance to erupt and everything to move backwards through time and return to her—the quickness in her womb with a kick, the sprawling out of these boys' limbs and hair, with her at the center of their lives again, mother mother mother. They thought she sat there waiting for sinew and bone to reconnect and blood to flow again to their brains and balls and toes so that when she stared at the neck she would see the rhythmic quiver of the full-to-bursting artery. A miracle, *Just give her a damned miracle already,* the sentimental ones half-prayed, exasperated and impatient, *Give her the miracle and be done with it,* as they hurried across the bridge and shivered. They thought that miracles are what teach you that life is deathless.

But it was never a miracle she wanted. She says as much now to the turkey vulture she beats within an inch of its life, but allows to fly, then tosses out a dried scrap of meat for it, and it returns, bent-winged—she pets its barnacled head. She steals a glance toward the river where she once saw the heron in the shape of the outboard motor. She didn't want the macabre dance, the bodies up and walking again, loosening their floppy necks from the ropes, as if everything could simply be as it was before. A forceful miracle, an erasure: rain wiping it all clean and clear. It's not that she didn't want them to live, but she did not want the Return, she could not believe in it—not when there was now transfiguration and change, radioactivity, half-lives, and half again.

She taps and tiptoes and flusters around, not quite sure what she wants now, but she thinks she might know—what is it, writhing in her mind?

If not rain, what is it she has wanted?

If not miracle, then mutter.

If not rain, then dew.

The dew.

Why?

Because she longs for surprise.

But why the dew?

Because she is nobody and nothing, and she remembers once waking on her smooth rock and sweeping the horrid curtain of her hair to the side and the dew fell on her face. And she ran to the reeds, keen; she searched hungrily for it with her laser eyes, her flamed face with its transfigured lines. Yes, it was something specific she wanted, she has not forgotten how to want, and she wants it now. She peered into the reeds and examined their long husky stems, so thirsty, and there: a bead of water condensing from the air, a tiny droplet—and she could feel the

Beneath of the reed's rough skin, the moisture inside, stirred, called out to meet, being drawn forth. This dew. It is the lighter kiss; it cannot heroically douse the flames; it's helpless, really, but it awakens what's within to help the stem bear the burning.

It is dew meeting dew. It is the answering, like when you rise from weeping. It does not soak, but asks. It is only intimation, the murmur, the smaller voice not so clear, only a mutter, someone in a bad mood, someone trying to speak through stones in the mouth. Dew mumbles, *Rise and Meet,* and—what surprise—the inside dew, the inside morning, the quench within the thirst itself.

But the rains do come, the greedy barley fills out, and green sings at her, accosting, from all sides. All along the riverbank people gather to set a seal of approval on her as she wears the bridal dress (lilac chiffon with some beaded trimmings) and a silk headdress, and everyone applauds. There is a celebration. But Rizpah slips off during the wedding festivities, at the moment of the hardest downpour of rain and stands out in her soaked dress that she peels from her body. Her tough slick skin lets the water pour off, the rain does not penetrate, it is too hard and too fast. It does not call forth the months of mornings, each morning when the arousal let her know there was something inside, impossibly, though she was nothing and nobody, *because* she was nobody and nothing.

She returns to the smooth rock where the bodies used to hang, their only motion a tremble when she or the milky girl would run through the heather and duckweed and the air moved in their wake and rattled the bones, like wind chimes.

She had come looking for the lynx, she remembers. But you won't see a lynx, though you know it's there, crouching and purring, the tender engine in the throat: it's there in the brush calming the poor bear and the hyena and the glinty fox, and it's more real to her in its secret purring place than if it were to pound out of the reeds into the bald open and streak past. She will lie down on this smooth rock until morning, then go back to where they're all gathered for her. Right now she squats and fiddles with stones. She once saw the heron in the outboard motor, a great blue. She still does not know birds, or not many, but she knows which ones like dried tomato seeds and which ones would chitter like tiny girls in her hair before they finally slept, and which ones can take a stone to the chest and still wobble free to fly again, with strong little bird bones, terribly strong little bird hearts. She has no hair now since she cut it with the knife; she slips off her silk headdress and searches the crags until she finds the frizzy pink wig stuck in a crevice, still electric. She puts it on and lies back down on the bare stone, a bit cold without the goat-hair rug, and she moves as if making a snow angel, but of course there is no snow here. And soon, they come down from the weeping cherry branches and settle into her pink hair for the night, nesting behind her ears. The rain subsides, she does not sleep, she waits for something new.

Notes

"Without"

I am grateful to Alec Irwin for his study of Simone Weil's eating metaphor in "Devoured by God: Cannibalism, Mysticism, and Ethics in Simone Weil" (*Cross Currents,* Summer 2001). The Weil passages included in this essay are drawn from *Gateway to God* (Fontana Books, 1974), *Waiting for God* (Harper Perennial Modern Classics, 2009), and *Gravity and Grace* (Bison Books, 1997); and from *The Simone Weil Reader,* Edited by George A. Panichas (Moyer Bell, 1977).

"The Long Weeping"

Rizpah's story is mentioned in the Bible only in the verses quoted here as an epigraph, from 2 Samuel 21 (New Revised Standard Version). Her story is filled out somewhat more in midrashic literature, the rabbinic interpretive study of the Bible. Though I base this essay on the sketch of her story, I have of course imagined almost all of the details. For the subtle ideas lying between the dew and the rain, I am grateful to Avivah Gottlieb Zornberg for the work she has done in *The Murmuring Deep: Reflections on the Biblical Unconscious* (Schocken Books, 2009) with the verses: "He shall come to us as the rain" and "I will be as dew to Israel" (Hosea 6.3, 14.6). I am also grateful to the Jewish Women's Archive (jwa.org), to Diana Edelman for "Rizpah: Bible" and to Tamar Kadari for "Rizpah: Midrash and Aggadah."

Acknowledgments

The author gratefully acknowledges the journals and anthologies where these essays first appeared, often in a slightly different form:

"Prologue" (as "The Long Weeping") in *Appalachian Heritage*

"Woman with Spirits" in *Red Holler: An Anthology of Contemporary Appalachian Literature*; (as "Soul Catchers") in *The Oxford American: Best of the South*

"This Soul Has Six Wings" in *Portland Magazine*; *Dreams and Inward Journeys: A Rhetoric and Reader for Writers*; *Best American Spiritual Writing*

"Without" in *Cimarron Review*

"Cattle Guard" (as "The Cattle Guard") in *Belmont Story Review*

"Resurrection" (as "Boy in a Blue Sweatshirt") in *Image*

"A Good Day" in *The Literary Review*

"So Great a Cloud" in *Ruminate Magazine*

"The Helicopter" in *Cheat River Review*

"Reliable Outcome" in *Sou'wester*

"Litany for the Body" in *Ruminate Magazine*

"Work Ethic" in *Ruminate Magazine* (winner of the VanderMey Nonfiction Prize)

About the Author

Jessie van Eerden is the author of the novels *Glorybound* (WordFarm, 2012)—winner of *Foreword Reviews*' Editor's Choice Fiction Prize— and *My Radio Radio* (Vandalia Press, 2016). Her work has appeared in *Best American Spiritual Writing, The Oxford American, Willow Springs,* and other publications. Jessie holds an MFA in nonfiction from the University of Iowa and directs the low-residency MFA program at West Virginia Wesleyan College.

About Orison Books

Orison Books is a 501(c)3 non-profit literary press focused on the life of the spirit from a broad and inclusive range of perspectives. We seek to publish books of exceptional poetry, fiction, and non-fiction from perspectives spanning the spectrum of spiritual and religious thought, ethnicity, gender identity, and sexual orientation.

As a non-profit literary press, Orison Books depends on the support of donors. To find out more about our mission and our books, or to make a donation, please visit www.orisonbooks.com.

The publication of this book was made possible by the generous contribution of Brent Short.